LITERACY
AND THE
ARTS
FOR THE
INTEGRATED
CLASSROOM

LITERACY

AND THE

ARTS

FOR THE

INTEGRATED

CLASSROOM

Alternative Ways of Knowing

Nancy Lee Cecil ■ **Phyllis Lauritzen**
California State University, Sacramento   *California State University, Sacramento*

Longman
New York & London

**Literacy and the Arts for the Integrated Classroom:
Alternative Ways of Knowing**

Longman, 10 Bank Street, White Plains, N.Y. 10606

Associated companies:
Longman Group Ltd., London
Longman Cheshire Pty., Melbourne
Longman Paul Pty., Auckland
Copp Clark Pitman, Toronto

Senior acquisitions editor: Laura McKenna
Production editor: Linda W. Witzling
Cover design and illustration: Laurie Angel Sadis
Text art: Fine Line, Inc. and Christina Lee Cecil
Production supervisor: Richard Bretan

Library of Congress Cataloging-in-Publication Data

Cecil, Nancy Lee.
    Literacy and the arts in the integrated classroom : alternative
ways of knowing / Nancy Lee Cecil, Phyllis Lauritzen.
        p. cm.
    Includes bibliographical references (p.) and index.
    ISBN 0-8013-1096-2
    1. Language arts (Elementary)—United States. 2. Arts—Study and
teaching (Elementary)—United States. 3. Performing arts—Study and
teaching (Elementary)—United States. 4. Interdisciplinary approach
in education—United States. 5. Socially handicapped children-
-Education—United States. I. Lauritzen, Phyllis. II. Title.
LB1576.C39   1994
372.6'0973—dc20
                                                        93-23254
                                                        CIP

1 2 3 4 5 6 7 8 9 10-MA-9897969594

To Jane—who would have been delighted that we wrote this book

Each second we live is a new and unique moment of the universe,
a moment that never was before and never will be again.
And what do we teach our children in school?
We teach them that two and two make four and
that Paris is the capital of France.
When will we also teach them what they are?
We should say to each of them: Do you know what you are?
You are a marvel. You are unique.
In all the world there is no other child exactly like you.
In the millions of years that have passed,
there has never been another child precisely like you.
And look at your body—what a wonder it is!
Your legs, your arms, your cunning fingers, the way you move!
You may become a Shakespeare, a Michelangelo, a Beethoven.
You have the capacity for anything!
Yes, you are a marvel. And when you grow up,
can you then harm another who is, like you, a marvel?
You must cherish one another.
You must work—we must all work—
to make this world worthy of its children.

—Pablo Casals

Contents

Preface

A Greek sage was reputed to have mused, "Humans are not vessels to be filled, but fires to be kindled." Accordingly, as authors of *Literacy and the Arts for the Integrated Classroom* we are asking very different kinds of questions about what an integrated curriculum *can* and *should* do. The book is based on the work of cognitive psychologist Howard Gardner as well as our own integration of research and experience in developing innovative methods for creating curriculum that will, indeed, "kindle" young minds. Our goal in writing this unique text is to help teachers to enhance children's literacy development using a cross-curricular program of drama, song, dance, photography, art, and poetry. The arts are for every child, but an effective program that integrates literacy and the arts need not be costly or require extensive training. The arts can enhance literacy and tap linguistic, musical, logical-mathematical, spatial, bodily-kinesthetic, interpersonal, and intra-personal intelligence—all ways through which we believe that children can demonstrate their understanding of ideas.

Children in today's schools are widely diverse, coming from a variety of ethnic, linguistic, and cultural backgrounds. From this challenging heterogeneous garden, children at all stages of literacy development can find expression for their thoughts, values, ideas, and feelings through the arts. Due to their differing backgrounds, certain children may understand and express concepts better through art than they ever could through the written word; moreover, some children may understand and express themselves better through one particular art form than another. Music may speak with the greatest clarity to one child; to another, a painting conveys the strongest message; to yet another, poetry possesses the most intense appeal. Therefore, a wide range of media are presented in this text to convey concepts to a range of learners so that the individual underlying messages can come across. Fortunately, it seems clear that understanding through one art form tends to reinforce and enhance appreciation and understanding of other art forms. Additionally, if children experience an expression through the arts and relate that expression to literacy, both symbol systems are improved—children learn to sing a poem as well as read it; they add a dance sequence to a story they have read and it comes to life in a most memorable way. Through this blending and flowing across different communication systems, children actually generate new meanings and expand existing ones as they struggle to express themselves through a variety of media.

PURPOSE OF THIS BOOK

The purpose of this book is to explore some of the ways children from all cultures and linguistic groups can use the arts to enhance the more traditional literacy activities of reading, writing, listening, and speaking. The integration of these two broad areas can offer many innovative ways for teachers of literacy to provide their students with experiences that will allow them to master the basic skills needed for literacy and have a positive effect on their capacity for aesthetic appreciation, growth, and sensitivity. This capacity is critical because it allows children the freedom to express themselves and allows teachers another way to assess what children know. Just as importantly, the integration of literacy and the arts will provide for children who learn in diverse ways an avenue through which to express what is most salient to them. The following conceptual map illustrates the authors' concept of the arts as it will be used in this text to include needlework, carpentry, jewelry, folktales, murals—or any other conceivable expression of the human spirit.

The book is intended for preservice students of reading, language arts, and the fine arts, and for practicing teachers, who may or may not have previous experience or known talent in the arts, but who wish to explore with their students—whether native English speakers or not, whether gifted or at risk—alternative avenues by which children can express what they think and feel. The book is also for practitioners who wish to move toward an integrated literacy program because they appreciate the extent to which arts can lend joy, spontaneity, and a high degree of satisfaction to learning. Finally, the book will appeal to those teachers who agree with our approach, but need some practical ideas for integrating literacy and the arts, as well as to those in fiscally strapped schools where the arts have been dropped, or are merely considered "frills" to be presented once or twice a week by a specialist.

ORGANIZATION

Literacy and the Arts is divided into three sections. Part 1, Foundations, begins with two chapters that present the research base and theoretical rationale for integrating literacy and the arts. Also included in this section are chapters on creativity and visualization, with a wide array of suggestions for developing an environment that encourages expression and appreciation of the arts. In Part 2, Expression, we explore the ways in which children can respond to their world through the joyous avenues of song, drama, poetry, photography, studio art, and dance by describing numerous activities for classroom use. Part 3, Appreciation, presents a wealth of

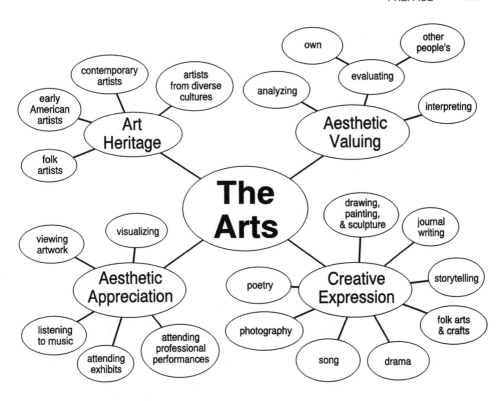

ideas on how children can be guided to feel comfortable with and enjoy classical music and art. We believe that by providing children with frequent exposure to art and music, and ample opportunities to talk about their personal reactions to selected works, their natural interest in expressing themselves will increase and they will begin to understand that there are a variety of ways to symbolize thoughts, experiences, and perceptions. To that end, the authors have attempted to make the experiences offered in art appreciation an expansion of options for children leading to freedom to experiment as well as a celebration of a host of different cultural artistic traditions.

IMPORTANT FEATURES

The content and the organization of *Literacy and the Arts for the Integrated Classroom* have been specifically crafted to make it as "user friendly" as possible. To meet this objective, we have included the following features in each chapter:

- An introduction to provide a mental set for reading the chapter and a framework for the ideas that will follow.
- Classroom vignettes to help readers envision how the ideas contained in the chapter were conceived, or how they might look in real classrooms.

- *Ideas for Classroom Practice* as guidelines for implementing an integrated literacy and the arts program.
- *Summaries* for a quick recap of the key ideas in each chapter.
- *Questions for Journal Writing and Discussion* to help readers internalize and think critically about key ideas in the text and help them relate new concepts to their own experiences.
- *Suggestions for Projects* to provide specific ways to become more familiar with the various disciplines of drama, song, dance, photography, art, classical music, and poetry.
- A *Bibliography of Children's Literature about the Arts* in the Appendix. These carefully chosen selections provide additional tools for using children's literature for a program that integrates literacy and the arts.

ACKNOWLEDGMENTS

We are grateful to a number of people for their help in getting this book written. Gary Cecil read and reread drafts; he also offered invaluable feedback from the perspective of a former teacher. Harry Lauritzen, too, listened, read and reread drafts, and served as "computer consultant" for the duration of this lengthy project. We could not have written this book without the patience and support of both.

The whimsical drawings of children performing various acts of artistic expression were created by Christina Lee Cecil, the eight-year-old daughter of one of the authors. Jo Anne Breese typed cheerfully through many revisions. Finally we wish to express our appreciation to the following reviewers, whose helpful suggestions and insight contributed greatly to the development of this book:

J. Estill Alexander, University of Tennessee, Knoxville
Stan Bochtler, Buena Vista College
Marietta Castle, Western Illinois University
Linda Clary, Augusta College
Gene Cramer, University of Illinois, Chicago
Judith Fueyo, Pennsylvania State University
Mary Anne Hall, Georgia State University
Victoria Chou Hare, University of Illinois, Chicago
Jose Salvadore Hernandez, Cal State, San Bernardino
Reta Hicks, Western Kentucky University
Dennis Kear, Wichita State University
Barbara Kiefer, Columbia University
Rebecca Kirshner, Ohio State
Linnea Lilja, University of Missouri
Pennie Olson, National-Louis University
Michon Rozmajzl, Boise State University
Lois Silvernail, Spring Hill College
Marylou Sorenson, University of Utah

PART I

Foundations: Integrating Literacy and the Arts

CHAPTER 1

A Developmental Perspective on Literacy and the Arts: Alternative Ways of Knowing

"I don't need theories; I want ideas I can use in the classroom" is a statement often made by teachers. It is true that teachers need ideas, but the basis for the selection of those ideas and the continuity or discontinuity of the resulting curriculum mean the difference between integrated developmental learning for children and scattered one-time experiences. Sound educational practice is always based on theory; the two cannot be separated. Disconnected day-to-day survival practitioners see no value in formal structured theories, which they view as academic inventions of no practical use. But is this true? What is the function of theory? An insightful, well-developed theory can lead to different perspectives—new ways of viewing behaviors and situations. In place of reaction to daily events, it can offer an opportunity for reflection and understanding of experiences. Educational practice then becomes a series of interrelated growth-enhancing experiences that promote learning for both children and teachers.

This book presents a developmental perspective on literacy and the arts based on an integration of theory and research. The suggested approach to literacy learning not only provides for intellectual learning and aesthetic development but also is ideally suited for stimulating the intrinsically motivated growth of the child intellectually, socially, and emotionally.

THEORETICAL FOUNDATIONS

Intellectual Development

Jean Piaget, through his clinical research on children's thought processes, has made us acutely aware that children are not "miniature adults." They think differently, moving through qualitative changes on their paths to maturity (Gruber & Vonèche,

3

1977). School-age children are making the transition from the preoperational stage of development (ages 2–6) to the concrete operational stage (ages 7–11). The central achievement of the preoperational period is the ability to form mental images, which allows children to think of and imagine objects and events not physically present. In the concrete operational stage, the child becomes capable of mental actions or representations that are reversible, relying, however, on concrete objects that are physically present. From Piaget's theory it follows that to support mental growth children need learning environments where they engage in hands-on activities with interesting objects and are provided with real-life experiences; those objects and experiences become the basis for stored mental images and mental representations. A literacy program based on the arts provides opportunities to integrate mental representations symbolically and use them in drama, art, storytelling and retelling, poems and prose, movement and dance, and music. Different symbol systems are utilized to represent ideas and experiences, and intellectual development is fostered in fun ways that are motivating and interesting to children.

According to Piaget (1985), children acquire new knowledge through the process of constructivism; they only truly understand that which they discover or interpret for themselves based on their experiences and their current levels of cognitive development. Mental growth is activated by states of disequilibrium between the child's concept of reality and the physical or social environment. The child, needing to make sense of the world, strives to resolve the conflict, and growth occurs through a process called *equilibration*. If, as Piaget stated, children must actively be involved in constructing their own knowledge, then passive, rote memorization and disconnected skill learning do not promote mental growth. The development and functional use of skills in expressive play and projects promote children's participation and the integration of new knowledge in meaningful ways.

Howard Gardner in his book *Frames of Mind* (1983) has developed a new theory of intelligence based on extensive research. Rather than consider intelligence a single unitary ability, Gardner hypothesizes seven intelligences:

1. Linguistic: the ability to use language to excite, please, convince, stimulate, or convey information;
2. Musical: the ability to enjoy, perform, or compose a musical piece;
3. Logical-mathematical: the ability to explore patterns, categories, and relationships by manipulating objects or symbols, and to experience in a controlled, orderly way;
4. Spatial: the ability to perceive and mentally manipulate a form or object, to perceive and create tension, balance, and composition in a visual or spatial display;
5. Bodily-kinesthetic: the ability to use fine and gross motor skills in sports, the performing arts, or arts and craft production;
6. Interpersonal: the ability to understand and get along with others;
7. Intrapersonal: the ability to gain access to and understand ones's inner feelings, dreams, and ideas. (Hatch & Gardner, 1988, p. 38)

Gardner (1983) defines an intelligence as "the ability to solve problems or to create products that are valued within one or more cultural settings" (p. x).

Different cultures value different intelligences. In Eskimo cultures spatial intelligence is valued because noticing subtle differences in snow and ice surfaces is critical to survival. In the Anang society of Nigeria, by the age of five children can sing hundreds of songs, play many percussion instruments, and perform complex dances. Musical and bodily-kinesthetic intelligence is promoted and encouraged in the Anang society (Armstrong, 1987). In our society, schools in the past have focused on two intelligences—linguistic and logical-mathematical—thus limiting the chances for success and feelings of achievement to children whose abilities lie in these areas. The redefinition of intelligence and the opportunity for children to develop their potentials through experiences in an expanded view of literacy and the arts could redefine not only intelligence but also the function and the relevance of school in the lives of children from a variety of backgrounds and cultures.

Social Development

Lev Vygotsky, the Russian psychologist and researcher, spoke of the social formation of the mind (Wertsch, 1985). He theorized that higher mental functions such as thought, language, and volitional behavior are formed through social interactions and result in the transmission of culture. Growth occurs when input from others is within a child's *zone of proximal development*, defined as "the distance between a child's actual developmental level, as determined by independent problem solving, and the higher level of potential development, as determined through problem solving under adult guidance or in collaboration with more capable peers" (Vygotsky, 1978, p. 86). If such social interactions are important, then the classroom environment must stimulate discussions about literature, favorite paintings and photographs, and most-loved music. It should provide opportunities for conversations while working on dramatizations, art projects, and the authoring of books. Since the arts are open-ended and generate individual responses with no single right answer, they encourage participation and interaction. Everyone can contribute and discover a voice or medium for their thoughts, reactions, and ideas (Eisner, 1992).

Emotional Development

Erik Erikson's theory of the Eight Stages of Man (1950) defines developmental issues that all humans face and must resolve as they progress through their life spans. From birth through 12 years of age, the successful resolution of developmental issues would cultivate in children feelings of basic trust, autonomy, initiative, and industry. Based on Erikson's theory, it is apparent that school experiences can have a tremendous impact on children's emotional learnings. Developmentally appropriate practice in school settings would promote trusting cooperative relationships rather than competition, support autonomy rather than conformity, plan for child-chosen and child-initiated activities whenever possible, encourage industry by focusing on attainable goals, and foster the appreciation of individual differences. A curriculum based on the integration of art, music, dance, and drama and a creative literacy program has the potential to make school and learning an exciting, fulfilling experience for all children.

A Developmental Progression Perspective

Recently, Gardner (1989) has connected theory and research to divide the developmental progression in the first half of life into five broad phases, the first two of which build the foundations for the third phase of middle childhood, the primary focus of this text. Each phase illuminates a social sphere, a form of knowledge to be obtained, and an educational regimen for facilitating that knowledge.

Phase 1—Infancy: Period of Sensory and Motor Knowledge. This is the sphere in which the infant operates in his or her own world, including relation to parents. The formation of Piaget's basic categories of space, time, object concept, other incipient concepts, and numerical sense are the focus. The sensory and motor aspects of intelligence develop with educational regimens of play, exploration, and practice.

Phase 2—Early Childhood: Period of Exploration and the Emergence of Cognitive Inclinations. The sphere of operation in this phase is the immediate family, neighbors, or relatives. The characteristics of this phase are acquaintance with the rules of different symbol systems (language, music, picturing, gesture, number) and competence obtained without direct instruction. The emergence of these multiple intelligences is facilitated by rich and varied exposure.

Phase 3—Middle Childhood: Period of Skill-building and School. The social sphere becomes peers and the local community. Basic literacies and notational knowledge are acquired. The task is to connect sensory and practical experiences to the culture's symbol system and to acquire an introduction to domains of knowledge through an educational program that emphasizes the acquisition of basic literacies and specialization in one art, one academic, and one physical activity.

According to Gardner's synthesis, there is a predictable progression of development, and the developmental task during the years of middle childhood is to connect sensory and practical experiences to the culture's symbol systems. The intent of this book, based on this theoretical foundation, is to make these connections by expanding traditional conceptions of the arts and literacy.

OUR THEORETICAL RATIONALE: A SYNTHESIS

The theories of human development reviewed speak to various aspects of development—social, emotional, and intellectual (remember: seven areas of intelligence). However, human development is not compartmentalized into such sections. Human development consists of various aspects of experiences integrated into a unique whole person. This text, therefore, is based on an integration and synthesis of the discussed developmental theories.

The authors maintain a theory that there are alternative ways of knowing and alternative paths to learning. Any program that recognizes and celebrates these differences must:

1. recognize that knowledge is constructed through the interactions of the perceptions and the awareness of the individual at his or her present developmental level and the quality of intellectual, physical, emotional, and social experiences provided by the environment;
2. acknowledge that prior knowledge and experiences influence the child's zone of proximal development;
3. value the child as an individual with the right to be, think, and feel as he or she does at this particular moment in time;
4. expand the child's awareness and provide options to develop the child's strengths and feelings of self-competence and self-worth;
5. provide a blend of developmentally appropriate experiences including child-initiated spontaneous play, child-chosen projects, and teacher-initiated age-appropriate curriculum experiences in the arts with options for child choice;
6. connect the child's sensory and practical experiences with the culture's symbol systems in creative nonthreatening ways;
7. promote student growth and self-evaluation through assessment efforts that document the learning of students through the maintenance of portfolios, the preparation of exhibitions, participation in projects, and reflective journal writing that crystallizes experiences (Chittenden, 1991);
8. teach literacy not as a skill consisting of isolated bits and pieces learned to please adults and to obtain grades on a report card, but as a tool to be used meaningfully in problem solving and real-life experiences; and
9. provide integrating experiences that teach the interrelatedness of knowledge rather than the segregation of knowing into separate curriculum areas and disciplines.

There has been concern that when children begin their scholastic careers, creativity is often lost and imagination stifled (Gardner, 1990). In schools, Eisner (1983) maintains that the arts are seen as opportunities for self-expression, not intellectual development. He claims, however, that the senses are integral parts of cognition. Forms of representation are related to conceptions, and there are differences between a rule governed and a figurative syntactical structure. He asks: "To what extent do children who work in the arts expand their ability to enjoy complexity, cope effectively with uncertainty, and tolerate ambiguity? What disposition does a 'back to basics' curriculum whose syntax is virtually all rule governed endanger in the young?" (p. 26). Rather than go back to basics, education should allow children to move forward to the future.

SUMMARY

An integration of the theories of Piaget, Gardner, Vygotsky, and Erikson provides a foundation for a curriculum that expands traditional conceptions of schooling. Literacy and the arts interface to present a range of alternative paths to learning so that the uniqueness of each child is respected and celebrated. This text addresses the need to reconcile and connect young children's educational experiences with their individual styles of learning and ways of making sense of the world so that all children are supported in developing their potentials.

QUESTIONS FOR JOURNAL WRITING AND DISCUSSION

1. Is there a theory that has influenced your educational practice? Name the theory and discuss how and in what ways it changed your perspectives and your ways of working with children.
2. Does Vygotsky's zone of proximal development apply only to children? Can you give a personal experience when you learned something under the guidance of another person?
3. Of Howard Gardner's seven intelligences, which do you feel are your strongest areas? Remember, we all have combinations of these elements. Provide examples, based on your natural predispositions, of both easy and difficult learning experiences you had as a child in elementary school.

SUGGESTIONS FOR PROJECTS

1. It has been stated that schools emphasize linguistic and logical-mathematical intelligence. Observe for at least two hours in an elementary classroom. Develop a grid with the seven intelligences along the side and mark the children engaging in activities that use various intelligences. Prepare a report in either written or oral form that includes a description of the classroom, grade level, your findings, and an analysis of their implications.
2. Basing his ideas on Gardner's theory of multiple intelligences, Thomas Armstrong (1987) gives an example of seven ways of completing an open-ended homework assignment for a unit on bird study. His suggestions follow:
   - Linguistic: book reports, oral presentations, writing compositions, tape recordings;
   - Spatial: charts and maps of a bird's migration patterns, pictures of birds;
   - Kinesthetic: hiking to a bird's natural habitat, building a replica of a bird's nest;
   - Logical-mathematical: collecting statistics about birds, answering the basic question: "how does a bird fly?";
   - Musical: finding records or tapes of bird calls and learning to imitate them;
   - Interpersonal: volunteering in a community project designed to safeguard the welfare of the local bird population;
   - Intrapersonal: creating a special place of solitude in nature for bird-watching. (p. 67)

   Prepare another open-ended project and list seven ways of fulfilling the assignment.

REFERENCES

Armstrong, T. (1987). *In their own way*. New York: St. Martin's Press.
Chittenden, E. (1991). Authentic assessment, evaluation, and documentation of student performance. In Vito Perrone (Ed.), *Expanding Student Assessment* (pp. 22–31). Alexandria, VA: Association for Supervision and Curriculum Development.

Erikson, E. (1950). *Childhood and society*. New York: Norton.

Eisner, E. (1983). On the relationship of conception to representation. *Art Education, 36*, 22–27.

Eisner, E. (1992). The misunderstood role of the arts in human development. *Phi Delta Kappan, 73*, 591–595.

Gardner, H. (1983). *Frames of mind*. New York: Basic Books.

Gardner, H. (1989). Balancing specialized and comprehensive knowledge: The growing educational challenge. In Thomas Sergiovanni & John Moore (Eds.), *Schooling for tomorrow: Directing reforms to issues that count* (pp. 148–165). Boston, Allyn & Bacon.

Gardner, H. (1990). *Art education and human development*. Los Angeles: The J. Paul Getty Trust.

Gruber, H., & Vonèche, J. (Eds.). (1977). *The essential Piaget*. New York: Basic Books.

Hatch, T., & Gardner, H. (1988). How kids learn: What scientists say. *Learnings, 17*(4), 36–39.

Piaget, J. (1985). *The equilibration of cognitive structures: The central problem of intellectual development*. Chicago: University of Chicago Press.

Vygotsky, L. S. (1978). *Mind in society*. Cambridge: Harvard University Press.

Wertsch, J. (1985). *Vygotsky and the social formation of mind*. Cambridge: Harvard University Press.

CHAPTER 2

The Context: Integrating Theory and Practice

"I really want to teach these kids, but how? They are at so many different levels. Some don't even speak English. It's hard to know what to do." These comments are from a conversation overheard in the teachers' lounge. This text suggests what might be done: Create an environment where children develop aesthetic and literate knowledge in supportive surroundings. This environment would consist of positive interactions between students and teachers and between students and peers; a curriculum to facilitate the growth of multiple intelligences; experiences to promote feelings of competency and self-worth; and a physical setting that buttresses this learning.

ENVIRONMENTAL MESSAGES

Just as body language often communicates more than oral language, environmental messages communicate true feelings better than linguistic rhetoric. Particularly for children, who are perhaps more sensitive to their physical surroundings than many adults, the environment often speaks in the following ways:

- Interaction between children is encouraged (the children's chairs and tables are grouped in sets of four);
- Children's art is celebrated (it is tastefully matted and displayed);
- Purposeful work is valued (materials and equipment are within reach and attractively displayed, and thought has been given to suitable workplaces and effective storage).

Maria Montessori (1967), the Italian educator, believed children absorbed their environment. The teacher's concerted attention to the provision of an age-appropriate environment is crucial. Such an environment supports the functional use of space and chooses beautiful and harmonious materials for the children's use, thus speaking to the importance the teacher places on developing different competencies, interactions, and awarenesses.

R. A. Smith (1992) has developed a theoretical scheme for learning in the arts built on five phases of aesthetic learning. These phases proceed from simple exposure and familiarization in the elementary grades to more demanding historical, appreciative, and critical studies in later grades.

Phase 1: Perception of Aesthetic Qualities (K–3).   Young children are sensitive to simple sensory and expressive qualities of all sorts of things, whether in nature, in objects used in daily life, or in works of their own making. Schools should cultivate a delight in the looks, sounds, tastes, and smells of the immediate environment and also direct attention to artworks. Thus, the job of creating dispositions toward aesthetic qualities gets underway.

Phase 2: Development of Perceptual Finesse (Grades 4–6).   Children of this age can perceive greater complexity in works of art. They begin to acquire a vocabulary or language for talking about art and its various elements. Relevant biographical and historical information can be included as well as works from other cultures.

Phase 3: Development of a Sense of Art History (Grades 7–9).   Curriculum becomes more formal and a survey of art history leads to an appreciation of the artistic traditions of different cultures.

Phase 4: Exemplar Appreciation (Grades 10–11).   Appreciation and in-depth study of works of art from Western and non-Western cultures become the focus of attention. Contextual factors as background, but not as the primary emphasis, can be included.

Phase 5: Critical Analysis (Grade 12).   Opportunities to fashion personal philosophies of art and to consider the question of artistic value and worth culminate the school curriculum for fostering aesthetic learning.

This scheme underscores the importance of the environment starting in the early years of schooling. The teacher can effect the environment positively in the following ways:

1. Mount and display children's artwork.
2. Offer a variety of quality tapes and records at the listening center and for use during group times.
3. Celebrate fine art by hanging examples of great artists' work at children's eye level.
4. Furnish a rich array of quality art materials and quality musical instruments (not homemade ones) for children's use.

5. Above all, provide a proliferation of children's books representing different genres of text and containing beautiful illustrations that use various art styles and media.

These are just a few of the many opportunities to speak powerfully to children through the environment. Learning environments are created by teachers and become part of all who experience them.

CURRICULUM EXPERIENCES

In tandem with the physical environment, the age and stage of the child determine the appropriate learning goals and methodology. Young children learn best by exploring and attempting to make sense of the wonderful world of people and things. They gradually develop talents and skills that can then be integrated and used in various ways to accomplish different goals. For preschool children, spontaneous play in a rich, age-appropriate environment facilitates learning and gradual growth in knowledge, skills, dispositions, and feelings (Katz & Chard, 1989). For school-age children, there is the goal of continued development in these areas and the use of those learnings in culturally appropriate ways.

A sequential path to elementary-age children's development in literacy and the arts, which is the focus of this text, emphasizes child-initiated spontaneous play as the learning medium in early childhood. This play expands in the elementary school to also include the use of teacher-facilitated child-chosen projects and teacher-initiated curriculum experiences in the arts with options for child choice. The emphasis of the teacher's role varies in the different educational settings, from preparing a rich environment for play, to scaffolding child-chosen projects, to teaching and apprenticeship relationships that validate, appreciate, and integrate children's innate wisdom and desire to learn.

The remainder of this chapter first focuses on the function of play in early childhood and then gives the rationale for the use of a project approach for more mature learners. Chapters 5 through 12 provide specific curriculum experiences in the arts.

THE ROLE OF PLAY IN BUILDING THE FOUNDATION FOR LITERACY AND ARTISTIC DEVELOPMENT

Julie is feeding her teddy bear a pretend lunch of ice cream and cake. Russell rushes to the easel during activity time in kindergarten to paint his current conception of a boy. Both Julie and Russell are demonstrating not only pretend play and creative uses of their imaginations but also the use of their inner mental representations of images and events in the outside world. These mental images are necessary for linguistic development, for symbolic representations in art, and for the comprehension of written text. In spontaneous pretend play, young children substitute images, symbols, or objects for reality. In fact, the period of children's play between the ages of 2 and 7 has been designated by Jean Piaget as the symbolic play period (Piaget, 1962). The spontaneous symbolic play of young children is a multifaceted avenue for emerging development. The following sections trace the development in three specific areas of play that are particularly relevant to literacy and the arts: speech play, painting with tempera, and dramatic and sociodramatic play. A knowledge of the normal sequence of children's development along with perceptive observation of each child provides the basis for planning experiences within the child's zone of proximal development.

Speech Play

Speech play begins with the infant's spontaneous play with phonology in which the infant practices the wide spectrum of sounds available for use in creating words. The babbling infant's repetitive "ma-ma-ma-ma-ma" is invested with meaning by adults and becomes the word *mama*, designating a particular person.

As children grow and gain mastery over the production of sounds, their explorations with the words, intonations, and rhythm of language continue as shown in creative monologues often developed to accompany dramatic play. Rachel, aged 3, persuades her doll to eat by saying, "Come on, baby, you have to eat lunch. Get-ta-ga-go-goo. Get-ta-goo-goo-goo. Shh! now she's asleep."

Speech play becomes more social as children mature and relate to peers. Joint conversations with creative back-and-forth turns delight participants (Cecil, 1990). The following 4-year-old boys developed their own contemporary counting rhyme using television channels as the stimulus.

MICHAEL: I hate channel four, I open the door. On channel five, a beehive.

JARED: No, it goes like this: On channel one, I suck my thumb. On channel two, Scoobydoo. On channel three, I suck my knee. On channel four, there's many more. On channel five, a beehive. On channel six, more tricks. On channel seven, I go to heaven. On channel eight, I make a mistake. On channel nine, Frankenstein. On channel—what? [*Looking over at Michael, who is making faces.*]

MICHAEL: On channel eleven . . .

JARED: No, on channel nine, Frankenstein. On channel ten, a big fat hen.

MICHAEL: No, on channel nine, I eat some slime. Ha ha ha.

JARED: It doesn't really go that way. It doesn't go any way. I just made it up.

MICHAEL: I did, too. I knew it.

This inborn fascination with the rhyme, rhythm, and patterns of language as evidenced by spontaneous speech play provides practice with the sounds and forms of language and contributes to the children's appreciation of poetry read aloud to them. This creative use of language by both the children themselves and the authors of books read to them promotes intuitive knowledge that the young schoolchild will later be encouraged to consider in a more conscious, analytical way (Lindfors, 1987). Speech play in early childhood provides a natural foundation for the development of the formal aspects of language study in the elementary school.

Painting with Tempera

The tempera paintings that young children produce go through a predictable universal sequence of development starting with exploration of the medium, followed by exploration of the use of space, progressing to the presymbolic stage when paintings are named *after* they have been painted (a Rorschach-type test), and finally reaching the symbolic stage when mental images are activated and thought is given to what to paint before the painting is started although the specific features depicted will evolve in the process of painting. Figure 2-1 graphically presents these stages.

If a young child of elementary school age states, "I can't draw," and refuses to try, the solution is not to teach the child to draw, but to provide the experiences and facilitative adult responses that may have been lacking in previous years (Gross, 1983). Providing such a child with access to creative materials and the freedom to explore while validating the child's creations will foster the child's joyful progression through the universal stages of children's art to the symbolic stage. In the symbolic stage mental images are used to portray people, objects, and events in the real world. Russell's drawing of a boy (Figure 2-1, #6), for example, indicates an ability to symbolize, through art, his internal schema and awareness of some of the details of a human figure. Symbolic representations form the basis not only for art but also for the comprehension and understanding of concepts and language.

Dramatic and Sociodramatic Play

Julie, the young child mentioned earlier in this chapter, was engaging in dramatic play when she fed her teddy bear lunch. Dramatic play is a form of symbolic play that occurs when objects and actions symbolize or substitute for reality. In dramatic play children take on the role of someone else, and when the play is carried out with another role-player with verbal interactions, it becomes sociodramatic play. Sara Smilansky (1968) maintains that sociodramatic play is the most highly developed form of symbolic play and contributes to the development of creativity, social skills, language, intellectual growth, and the child's integration of the culture and mores of the adult world.

A literacy-rich dramatic play area would include pencils and paper for waiters and waitresses to write customers' orders in a restaurant that has a printed menu and alongside the print a matching rebus menu; magazines, newspapers, and books in the playhouse; prescription pads for a doctor's office; signs for stores; note pads for a refrigerator door; stationery, envelopes, and stamps for letters to be written and delivered to the addressee; and any reading and writing materials applicable to the real-life situations being dramatized. In such an environment "pretend" writing and "pretend" reading flourish.

UNIVERSAL STAGES OF DEVELOPMENT IN CHILDREN'S PAINTING

1. Exploration -
   Linear

2. Exploration -
   Circular

3. Extended Use
   of Space

4. Enclosure
   of Space

5. Pre-Symbolic

6. Symbolic

FIGURE 2.1

SOURCE: From Phyllis Lauritzen, "Facilitating Integrated Teaching and
Learning in the Preschool Setting: A Process Approach," *Early
Childhood Research Quarterly,* 7(4), 531–550. Copyright 1992
by Ablex Publishing Corporation. Reprinted by permission.

Play's Contribution to Literacy and the Arts

In the past, it was thought that literacy began with the formal teaching of reading and writing skills in school. In recent years it has come to be recognized that literacy development starts in the early childhood years without formal instruction but is facilitated by a literacy-rich play environment including both physical resources and social mediation (Bissex, 1980; Clay, 1976; Goodman, 1986; Heath, 1983). The term *emergent literacy* has been coined to describe this process and emphasizes the interrelatedness of all the language arts of speaking, listening, reading, and writing (Teale & Sulzby, 1989).

In a literacy learning play environment, children learn the functions of literacy in real-life situations (Christie, 1991). Language is needed to play with peers, solve problems, participate in conversations, and share activities and trips with others. Experimentation with crayons, paints, pencils, and paper provides practice in graphics. Everywhere there is a great variety of printed materials, including signs, labels, newspapers, magazines, and, most importantly, books to enjoy and share and promote orthographic awareness. In such an environment young children are not "just playing"; they are developing the needed foundations to prepare themselves for the challenge of learning to read and write and become members of "the literacy club" (F. Smith, 1988).

For development in both emergent literacy and aesthetic awareness, the provision of an enriched play environment with opportunities to create—whether it be a painting, a rhythmic response to music, a chant developed while swinging, or an imaginative telling of a story—is essential. Such an environment allows children to explore without fear of evaluative judgments and to develop ever-expanding competencies in the integrated knowledge of the functional use of literacy in their world, and additionally promotes a joyful appreciation of the aesthetic qualities of life.

THE USE OF THE PROJECT APPROACH TO PROMOTE INTEGRATED LEARNING IN THE ELEMENTARY SCHOOL

"We did it!" Jim exclaimed, proudly demonstrating his feelings of competence, satisfaction, and community spirit following the successful production of *Jack and the Beanstalk* by a group of second graders. The production included a giant wearing platform shoes and a golden egg made from a gold-painted L'eggs hosiery carton. A room divider panel with painted scenery attached to it was moved by trolls (who were actually employees of the giant or "giant helpers") and used to change the location of the play from Jack's house to the giant's castle. Think of the enjoyment, the functional use of language, the cooperative problem solving, and the opportunities for creativity in the arts involved in such a child-chosen project!

In elementary school the context has changed to a classroom with perhaps 30 classmates. The child has matured and developed knowledge, skills, and talents that can now be used as tools for expanded learning opportunities. The focus of learning has shifted. The rules of the game have changed. In fact, the dominant play of this period, according to Piaget (1962), is games with rules. Real-world competencies replace the pretend world of the preschool years (Rubin, 1988). What those competencies are, how they are acquired, and how they are used become the focus of curriculum planning and implementation. The authors of this text discuss how these competencies might be learned and how they might be used in the following section on the project approach, suggested as one component of the elementary school learning environment that can be used in conjunction with teacher-initiated curriculum experiences to facilitate and integrate student learnings.

The Project Approach

The idea of learning through projects rather than separate subject teaching is a concept that has fluctuated in popularity over the past 50 years (Stewart, 1986). Both William H. Kilpatrick (1918) and John Dewey (1933) advocated the project approach because of its focus on active inquiry, discovery learning, and problem solving in a meaningful context for children. However, by 1975 Daniel Tanner and Laura Tanner reported that the project method was all but forgotten in educational literature and did not even appear in the *Handbook of Research on Teaching*. Today, as the pendulum swings back to integrated learning, thematic curriculum, developmentally appropriate practice, and the use of learning centers, the project approach has been reintroduced (Brewer, 1992; Katz & Chard, 1989). The project approach as a means of classroom management allows for child-initiated and teacher-guided learning, long-term planning and involvement, and skill learning embedded in experiences that are meaningful to children. Projects can be executed either by an individual working alone or in small heterogeneous groups working cooperatively. Moreover, the hands-on activities afforded by the project approach provide the best multisensory learning environments for second-language speakers.

Implementing a Project Approach

The following guidelines are suggestions for implementing a project approach in the elementary school:

1. Child-initiated projects are chosen through the spontaneous interest of the children in a topic or an area of study they have "discovered."
2. Teacher-initiated projects may be suggested by the teacher based on his or her knowledge of the lives, personal experiences, and developmental characteristics of the students. Even though the teacher may have initiated the project suggestions, it is the children who choose which of the projects will be their focus. Child choice is critical and fundamental to the project approach.
3. Once chosen by the students, the actual development of the project creatively evolves and is negotiated among participants.
4. The practical application of academic skills, such as reading to obtain needed information, writing to list job assignments, and calculating relevant mathematical problems, are integrated into the project through

the teacher's creative facilitation of an awareness of their potential usefulness to the project participants.

5. Because the project extends over a period of time, it requires long-range planning.

6. The teacher and the students constantly evaluate the project results, thus necessitating reflective problem-solving and critical thinking skills.

IDEAS FOR CLASSROOM PRACTICE

The following projects revisit the areas discussed in the role of play—speech play, painting with tempera, and dramatic and sociodramatic play—to demonstrate how differences in age characteristics interact with appropriate curriculum to facilitate development.

Projects That Involve Play with Language

Just as speech play assists in the phonological development of the emerging literate child, the extensive language play of the elementary-age child furthers language and literacy development in unique child-compatible ways. Children of this age exhibit obvious delight in jokes, puns, riddles, teasing rhymes, and the double meanings of words. Projects involving language play offer creative, fun roads to practice and obtain knowledge of the structure and meanings of words, and to stimulate literacy development.

The production of a humorous TV variety show is a project that could be suggested and, if selected by a group of children, would involve them in many decisions involving oral language, reading, writing, and creative staging. Decisions to be made would include arranging different segments of the program by categories, such as favorite riddles, knock-knock jokes, and puns; selecting material from books (Brown, 1987; Cerf, 1961; Rosenbloom, 1977); trying out the selected material on each other; and agreeing on what should be used in the program. Once selected, the back-and-forth dialogue of the jokes and riddles would require the participation of two performers. A skit based on an Amelia Bedelia book (Parish, 1977) could illustrate the double meaning of words and would necessitate a narrator, several players, plus props and scenery. Scripts could be written and elements timed to fit within the allotted program schedule, and commercials for the program's sponsor could be created.

The show might be presented to the class as well as other classes in the school and, if a video camera were available, it could actually be taped for future viewing. Imagine the laughter and enjoyment generated for performers and the audience by such a project!

At this age language play not only involves humor, but is also manifested in the childhood chants and jumprope rhymes that have been passed along from generation to generation. Recently, with the development of rap, a new form of rhythmic language play has been created. The audiotaping and transcription of the local favorites could become the text for a class book that could be illustrated by class artists. Existing chants could be used as templates for creating original ones; new raps could be developed.

An intrinsically motivated nonthreatening literacy learning environment starts with children's natural interest in language and language play, expands to include opportunities to indulge this interest in meaningful projects while interacting with peers, and provides for the use of academic skills within a meaningful context.

Art Projects

A preschool child spontaneously paints, enjoying the exploration of the medium and the process of painting. Later, as the child becomes more product oriented, the finished painting becomes the focus of attention. The teacher in the elementary school wishing to implement the project approach might use art as a stimulus to further literacy development for a child lacking in verbal or writing skills who might be better able to communicate by executing an imaginative painting. The teacher can encourage the child's emergent literacy development by asking the child, "Tell me about your painting." The reply can be written down by the teacher, who accepts and values what the child says and does not expect a story. Some children may be primarily interested in exploring the qualities of the colors and paint and creating a design (Dyson, 1988). Gardner (1979) refers to such children as *patterners*. Other children, labeled *dramatists*, seem much more interested in using the drawing as a prop for talking about an experience or telling a story. Both, however, observe their words being transcribed and often spontaneously attempt to read the text.

An alternative project for a talented artist might be to produce the illustrations for a wordless picture book and to have different classmates or groups write their version of the depicted story. For children who have not yet begun to speak in English, their stories could be expressed in their native language. What artist could resist wanting to read different stories written by fellow classmates inspired by the artist's own pictures?

It is common practice for teachers to provide the option of letting children respond to a piece of literature through art. However, in this text's approach to the arts and literacy, the individual's art becomes a creative stimulus for reading and writing rather than a response to a story written by someone else. Because the child's art provides the starting point for the project, the child is more likely to have an investment in the activity.

A group art project could evolve from the need for a mural for a class bulletin board based on, for example, a current thematic unit on dinosaurs. The artists responsible for this aspect of the project would have to research in books the background scene depicting the environment 100 million years ago. Others could volunteer to draw different dinosaurs to scale. For example, if a *Tyrannosaurus rex* was 30 feet tall, they could make it 30 inches tall for the mural. Labels would need to be made. A list of the various components of the project could be developed and volunteers' names could be written beside the listed jobs. Everyone who chose to work on the project could participate and contribute in self-selected ways. The cooperative effort would be a part of the classroom environment, a source of pride for all who worked on it, and the motivation for practicing and refining academic skills.

Drama Projects

Oral storytelling is a personal form of drama and can facilitate a natural child-compatible transition from home to school. Every day, children tell anecdotes, share memories, communicate feelings, and construct narratives. This is real-life drama, using a child's own expressive language as its base. Since many cultures value the oral language tradition, storytelling may already be a part of a child's repertoire. In a group setting in which adults and other children listen and even transcribe these stories, the experience validates a child in a very special way (Paley, 1990).

Courtney Cazden (1985) has suggested that show and tell or sharing time be reconceptualized. She asks the question "What is sharing time for?" and suggests it could be an opportunity for the sharing of self-chosen stories on out-of-school experiences. This sharing creates a sense of community. According to Cazden's research, the teacher's expectations for and appreciation of the child's oral sharing are crucial. An example of a teacher's facilitative response to a child's narrative follows:

> JERRY: Ummm, two days ago, ummm, my father and my father's friend were doing something over the other side, and my sister wanted, uhhh, my father's friend to make her a little boat out of paper, and the paper was too little. He used a dollar and, ummm, my sister undoed it and we, ahhh, bought my father and my mother Christmas presents.
>
> TEACHER: A man made a boat out of a dollar bill for you? Wow! That's a pretty expensive paper to use. (p. 182)

This teacher listened. Her goal was not to have storytelling serve as oral practice in the kind of English language usage in which children will be expected to write in future schoolwork, but to validate a child's contribution and build a sense of community.

Once children and the teacher have become comfortable with oral storytelling, a further expansion of the acquired skill through projects becomes possible. Stories can be written down for retelling and dramatization (Paley, 1990). Wordless picture books (Bruna, 1987; Collington, 1986; dePaola, 1981; Goodall, 1988; Krahn, 1977; McCully, 1987; Prater, 1987; Turkle, 1975; Winter, 1976) can encourage a variety of stories based on the same illustrations (Bromley, 1992). These can be taped and used at the listening center or transcribed and published to become part of the class library. Original narratives can be taped, analyzed by the storyteller, refined and edited, and, when the creator is satisfied, retaped for inclusion in a portfolio or to share with parents and classmates. The use of a simple prompt, such as "Once upon a time there was a poor prince who . . ." can stimulate group storytelling where each person takes a turn adding to the plot. The advantage of combining storytelling and the project approach is that the involvement for the child enhances self-esteem, furthers self-motivation, and stimulates growth in all facets of the language arts—speaking, listening, writing, and reading.

Additionally, with the elementary-aged child's increased attention span and ability to sustain interest over a period of time, the spontaneous dramatic play of the preschool years can become a project to produce a play that is planned, creatively produced, and presented to an audience. Such a project could be maintained over a period of a week, several weeks, or whatever time span is necessary and appropriate for the age of the children participating. While dramatizing a story read by the class is a technique frequently used by teachers to increase reading comprehension, the scenario for the play in this case would be selected by the group. This would involve the group in discussing the merits of different books to be dramatized and even reading different stories to make a selection. Once the selection is made there is much planning, decision making, problem solving, and negotiation required to produce the play. *All* areas of the arts are involved in listing the different characters, developing their lines, collecting props, printing programs, producing the play, and presenting it to an audience. The creation of scenery would be an artistic group project; other children might select musical themes to enhance the "mood" of their play; and an appropriate dance routine could be generated for the production. Every child's talents and abilities would be used, and everyone would contribute to the cooperative effort, thus bringing the entire spectrum of the arts into the project. The production of *Jack and the Beanstalk* at the beginning of this section was an example of such a project.

The Contribution of the Project Approach to Art and Literacy Learning in the Elementary School

The world of the preschool child's play is full of spontaneity, creativity, curiosity, and child-initiated activity. However, this world is often replaced in school with structured, teacher-directed activities that emphasize the serious business of learning the skills required for participation in society. Howard Gardner in his book *The Unschooled Mind: How Children Think and Schools Should Teach* (1991) offers a framework for understanding educational experiences and suggests the need for developmentally appropriate bridges to close the gap between children as learners and what needs to be learned.

The authors believe that such bridges are created in kindergarten and the elementary school by using the arts in play, projects, and age-appropriate curriculum experiences that provide choices for students. These experiences provide opportunities for the active acquisition of academic skills in functional child-motivating experiences. Moreover, there is an emphasis on cultivating not only creativity, respect, and empathy toward others, but also dispositions to continue personal learning. The learning of literacy within self-enhancing contexts and the use of acquired competencies in meaningful ways satisfy the requirements of modern schooling and at the same time provide for the extraordinary diversity of contemporary students.

SUMMARY

Children pick up on the environmental messages created by a teacher who values aesthetic learning and the creative and functional use of space. Working in tandem with the physical environment, developmentally appropriate curriculum provides opportunities to facilitate the growth of literacy through play, projects, and teacher-initiated learning experiences with options for child choice. Specific examples of play and projects operationalize the integration of theory and practice in this text's approach to the interface between literacy and the arts.

QUESTIONS FOR JOURNAL WRITING AND DISCUSSION

1. Montessori believed that children absorb their environment. Think about an environment where you spend a large amount of time. What messages are you absorbing from the physical environment? From the social environment?

2. What if a parent of a child in your classroom complained that the children are "just playing" and asked, "When are you going to teach my child some of the basics like the letters and sounds of the alphabet? She's going to first grade next year and I want her to be ready." How would you respond?

3. Think back to your own years in the elementary classroom. Can you recall any project that you worked on with classmates? What do you remember about the project? Looking back on the experience, what do you think were the teacher's learning objectives? Do you think those objectives were met? Why or why not?

SUGGESTIONS FOR PROJECTS

1. Visit a classroom and focus on the aesthetic qualities of the environment using the five features mentioned at the conclusion of the section "Environmental Messages." What other elements of the environment, both positive and negative, did you observe? What suggestions can you make for improving the aesthetic messages emanating from the classroom environment?

2. Visit a preschool and observe the play and the players, focusing on examples of speech play, painting with tempera, and dramatic or sociodramatic play. See if you can place the children on a developmental continuum based on the type of speech play, the stage of development of their paintings, and the quality of the dramatic or sociodramatic play.

3. Spend a morning in an elementary classroom and observe and record the types of experiences provided according to the following categories: teacher-directed group activities; teacher-planned learning centers; child-initiated activities; projects planned jointly by the students and the teacher. Create additional categories if necessary. Prepare a report or write in your journal on your findings, including the grade level observed, the number of students in the classroom, and comments on the children's participation and involvement in the different types of learning situations.

REFERENCES

Bissex, G. (1980). *GNYS AT WRK: A child learns to read and write*. Cambridge: Harvard University Press.

Brewer, J. (1992). *Introduction to early childhood education*. Boston: Allyn & Bacon.

Bromley, K. (1992). *Language arts: Exploring connections*. Boston: Allyn & Bacon.

Brown, M. (1987). *Joke book*. New York: Warwick.

Bruna, D. (1987). *A story to tell*. Los Angeles: Price/Stern/Sloan.

Cazden, C. (1985). Research currents: What is sharing time for? Language Arts, *62*(2), 182–188.

Cecil, N. (1990). Understanding play: An important precursor to literacy. *The California Reader, 23*, 16–18.

Cerf, B. (1961). *More riddles*. New York: Random House.

Christie, J. (1991). Play and early literacy development: Summary and discussion. In J. Christie (Ed.), *Play and early literacy development* (pp. 233–246). Albany: State University of New York Press.

Clay, M. M. (1976). *Young fluent readers*. London: Heinemann.

Collington, P. (1986). *Little pickle*. New York: Dutton.

dePaola, T. (1981). *The hunter and the animals*. New York: Holiday House.

Dyson, A. H. (1988). Appreciate the drawing and dictating of young children. *Young Children, 43*(3), 25–32.

Dewey, J. (1933). *How we think* (rev. ed.). Lexington, MA: Heath & Co.

Gardner, H. (1979) *Artful scribbles*. New York: Basic Books.

Gardner, H. (1983). *Frames of mind*. New York: Basic Books.

Gardner, H. (1991). *The unschooled mind: How children think and schools should teach*. New York: Basic Books.

Goodall, J. (1988). *Little red riding hood*. New York: McElderry.

Goodman, Y. M. (1986). Children coming to know literacy. In W. H. Teale & E. Sulzby (Eds.), *Emergent literacy: Writing and reading* (pp. 1–14). Norwood, NJ: Ablex.

Gross, L. (1983). Why Johnny can't draw. *Art Education, 36*(2), 74–77.

Heath, S. B. (1983). *Ways with words: Language, life, and work in communities and classrooms*. New York: Cambridge University Press.

Katz, L., & Chard, S. (1989). *Engaging children's minds: The project approach*. Norwood, NJ: Ablex.

Kilpatrick, W. H. (1918). The project method. *Teachers College Record, 19*, 390.

Krahn, F. (1977). *The mystery of the giant footprints*. New York: Dutton.

Lindfors, J. (1987). *Children's language and learning*. Englewood Cliffs, NJ: Prentice-Hall.

McCully, E. A. (1987). *School*. New York: Harper & Row.

Montessori, M. (1967). *The absorbent mind*. New York: Dell.

Paley, V. (1990). *The boy who would be a helicopter: The uses of storytelling in the classroom*. Cambridge: Harvard University Press.

Parrish, P. (1977). *Teach us, Amelia Bedelia*. New York: Greenwillow.

Piaget, J. (1962). *Play, dreams, and imitation in childhood*. New York: Norton.

Prater, J. (1987). *The gift*. New York: Viking/Penguin/Puffin.

Rosenbloom, J. (1977). *Doctor Knock-knock's official knock-knock dictionary*. New York: Sterling.

Rubin, K. (1988). Some "good news" and some "not-so-good news" about dramatic play. In D. Bergen (Ed.), *Play as a medium for learning and development*. Portsmouth, NH: Heinemann.

Smilansky, S. (1968). *The effects of sociodramatic play on disadvantaged children*. New York: Wiley.

Smith, F. (1988). *Joining the literacy club*. Portsmouth, NH: Heinemann.

Smith, R. A. (1992). Toward percipience: A humanities curriculum for art education. In B. Reimer & R. A. Smith (Eds.), *The arts, education, and aesthetic knowing*. Ninety-first yearbook of the National Society for the Study of Education (pp. 51–69). Chicago: University of Chicago Press.

Stewart, J. (1986). *The making of the primary school*. Philadelphia: Open University Press.

Tanner, D., & Tanner, L. (1975). *Curriculum development: Theory into practice*. New York: Macmillan.

Teale, W., & Sulzby, E. (1989). Emergent literacy: New perspectives. In D. Strickland & L. Morrow (Eds.), *Emerging literacy: Young children learn to read and write* (pp. 1–15). Newark, DE: International Reading Association.

Turkle, B. (1976). *Deep in the forest*. New York: Dutton.

Winter, P. (1976). *The bear and the fly*. New York: Crown.

CHAPTER 3

Creativity: An Essential Ingredient for Literacy and the Arts

When the terms *creative expression* and *imagination* are used, one generally thinks of the arts as providing the best examples of what the combination of the two might accomplish, since all art begins in the imagination and is then communicated through various modes of creative expression. These modes may be painting, music, drama, or a multitude of other forms. Even a small child's play that begins as a rudimentary activity with no specific content can be gradually filled with subject matter and then evolve fully into an artistic creation.

In fact, young children tend to make the transition between their inner and outer worlds easily, as they intuitively alternate between the symbolism of art and language in order to make sense of their world. It should be one of the major tasks of language, therefore, to ensure that children are free to explore both sets of symbols as they mature. To do this, fostering creative expression must be a priority. However, in a nation that continues to hold fast to standardized test scores to provide evidence that teachers are teaching and learners are learning, it appears that creativity, which cannot be rigidly measured, is not a commodity with the highest priority. As R. J. Sternberg and T. I. Lubart (1991) assert, "Clearly to engender creativity, first we must value it." Do we value creativity in this society? The answer is not a simple one.

DEFINING CREATIVITY

Unfortunately, the umbrella term *creativity* tends to be a highly charged, quasi-political concept. Many parents and educators fear that fostering creativity means that a teacher may be using a variety of progressive and greatly ennobling educational alternatives while perhaps giving less attention to such "mundane" areas as arithmetic, spelling, and the like. Such an interpretation merely underscores the confusion surrounding the term creativity, for much of the concern and negative reaction to the term stems from the fact that no one is truly certain what creativity is, although a constellation of definitions can be found in the literature. For example, creativity has been defined as "taking known bits of information and putting them together in a way that no one else has thought of before" (Calabria, 1977). The field of psychology asserts that "creativity is the idiosyncratic perception of new intellectual relationships never before experienced by the individual between two or more stimuli" (Scofield, 1960). On the other hand, the usually proffered pedagogical definition often suggests that creativity is a piece of artwork or writing that is aesthetically pleasing, clever, or simply "cute."

The term creativity is defined, for the purpose of this text, in a much broader sense to include a whole compendium of ways that children might freely express themselves. These ways might include a socially sensitive observation, a well-constructed question, as well as the more traditional creative expressions of artistically crafted products. Just how broadly creativity is defined is critical to any program planning, for far too often creative ideas are ignored, or worse yet, actively squelched when well-meaning educators are only watching for a creative product that matches their particular aesthetic standards. Thus, children quickly identify the teacher's creative agenda and soon begin to forgo their own artistic expression so that they may instead please the teacher.

SQUELCHING CREATIVITY

A recent informal study by one of the authors of this text underscores the child's quandary. The author, interested in exploring the nature of creativity, designed an informal experiment involving a "test" of creativity. She showed several children a small box and gave them these instructions: "I want you to think of as many things as you can that could be done with this box." To a similar group of six children she offered the following slightly modified directions: "I want you to try and think of as many clever and creative things as you can to do with this box. Only write down very creative, high-quality ideas." The result of this informal experiment, as you may have guessed, was that the first group of children, who were not creatively restricted and made intellectually self-conscious by having to monitor the quality of their ideas, came up with significantly more things to do with the box than the other group. And, ironically, that group's ideas were decidedly more imaginative and original—or "creative." The study makes the important statement about the elements that are most needed to foster creativity in the classroom: there must be a lack of self-consciousness, a knowledge that taking risks is actively encouraged, and an atmosphere of freedom to enable children to create without undue anxiety about how the other children—or the teacher—might perceive their product.

Similarly, another pervasive classroom routine that may actively inhibit creative thinking is the Initiation-Response-Evaluation (IRE) strategy that dominates most language arts discussions (Roller, 1989). Using this pattern, the teacher asks a question ostensibly designed to get the children ready to interact with what they are about to read. If, for example, the story to be read is about a little girl winning an award, the teacher might initiate a response by asking if any child in the class has ever won an award. Some child may then respond by mentioning that his father once told him that he won an award one time for touching his nose with his tongue at Boy Scout camp. At this point the teacher evaluates the child's response, comparing it with her own interpretation, culture, and "hidden agenda," thus controlling how the child's reply will be received. In this case, the teacher may very well fail to accept the nose-touching anecdote as a valid example of an award, as it may not compare favorably with the academic awards she has in mind. The child's reply is summarily dismissed. The child learns to try harder next time to match the teacher's meaning, thus repressing his own spontaneous and creative expression of ideas. Or, in many cases, the child decides that it is probably safer not to respond at all.

IDEAS FOR CLASSROOM PRACTICE

By contrast, an environment where risk taking is actively encouraged and personal expression is valued—no matter what form it may take—is best suited to the development of creativity. A risk-taking classroom can be developed in the following ways:

- *Value what is unique about each child.* Although the large numbers of children in most elementary classrooms makes a certain amount of conformity necessary, a teacher should always make it his or her business to find out what is truly special about each child. Academically, the teacher must begin to think beyond the traditionally accepted ways of expressing intelligence—in math and language—and be open to other expression through art, music, interpersonal, social, and practical skills, as well as physical expressions. Additionally, the teacher should make it clear that he or she values a child's personal statement, whether that statement is expressed via an unusual hairstyle, a unique way of making a lay-up shot, or an interesting manner of telling a joke.

- *Constantly stress that there is more than one answer to most important questions.* Because the rudimentary components of learning (timetables, for example) are so often on a purely factual level, children may unfortunately begin to believe that there is one "correct" answer to everything—even a correct way to sing a song, paint a picture, or write about their fantasies. Thus, for children to explore their own answers for self-expression, it is critical that they feel free not only to look at alternative solutions to questions, but also to look at the world in a variety of ways. A teacher can foster a sense of freedom by frequently asking, "Does anyone have a *different* idea about that?" or "Is there *another* way we could think about this?" while affirming a host of thoughtful responses.

- *Make sure that every creative effort, no matter how poorly executed, brings enough satisfaction to enable the child to want to try again.* Children have differing abilities across the compendium of creative arenas. They also differ in the experiences they bring to each area. Thus, if the teacher allows a great deal of variation in acceptable quality, especially at the initial stages of exploration, and actively appreciates the child's interest and effort in the creative process, the child will feel enough intrinsic satisfaction to want to repeat the activity. And, of course, practice with any creative expression, as in skiing, typing, or any other endeavor, inevitably leads to growth and thus to increased satisfaction.

- *Model creativity in as many ways as possible.* Many teachers possess some creative talents (especially if one accepts the previously proffered broad definition of the term), but teachers can be unduly modest. *All* creative aptitudes, no matter how meager, should be celebrated to show an avid appreciation for creativity when it is manifested by colleagues, world and national leaders, and most importantly, the students.

- *Heighten sensory awareness.* An atmosphere that has the best chance of giving rise to creativity, in all its forms, is one that abounds with the arts: soft classical music is played in the background and casually, but frequently, discussed; fine art paintings grace the periphery of the classroom and are introduced with zest; and good literature is read to the children and discussed with them on a daily basis.

William Schutz in his book *Joy* (1967) suggests that the creative process involves several stages, each stage building upon the preceding one. Each stage merges with other creative experiences until the final entity—a creative individual capable of rewarding self-expression—is realized. But in order to evolve creatively, Schutz warns, a child must be able to draw perceptions from a rich sensory environment. If children come from homes where these experiences have not occurred, it becomes even more critical for the teacher to provide the adequate stimuli for creative expression within the classroom.

- *Ask many questions requiring critical thinking but provide adequate "think time."* An atmosphere where creativity is best nurtured is one in which children are continuously stretched to think and respond beyond simple yes or no answers to questions. They must be provoked to deeply consider the teacher's questions and also the questions and comments of their classmates. Learning to think creatively takes place during the process of becoming sensitive to problems, deficiencies, gaps in knowledge, disharmonies, and the like. Thinking creatively involves bringing together new relationships from existing ones, making guesses, or formulating hypotheses about problems, testing them, retesting them, perfecting them, and then communicating the results. Clearly, it is a lengthy process that takes time. Therefore, teachers must become comfortable with moments of silence to give every child an opportunity to carefully think through their ideas and then formulate a response, especially children for whom English is a second language.

- *Never assign grades to creative work.* Assigning letter or numerical grades to any piece of personal authorship, especially if the grade is less than satisfactory, is one of the surest ways to thwart all future creative endeavors. Besides the obvious argument that "art is subjective" and cannot be absolutely evaluated, there is the deeper concern that a mediocre grade on a child's proud work may be profoundly damaging to that child's concept of himself or herself as creator. Thoughtful comments that address the creator's objectives are preferable, and the intellectual interchange is usually received graciously by the child. Portfolio assessment is gaining acceptance as a way to show progress or growth over time. In selected projects, students and teachers collaboratively use this approach to identify pieces of creative work. Then orally or in written form, the students answer questions about their selections, such as: "What was I trying to do?" "How did I select this piece of work for my portfolio?" "How do I feel it compares to other work I have done?" "What will I try next?" (California Department of Education, 1992). In this way, students gain ownership over the evaluation of their work and take the initiative in striving to improve it.

- *When sharing creative work, never single out the "best" or (heaven forbid) the "worst."* Again the teacher's is but a single subjective evaluation, and children must be allowed to create in the manner that their own heart, soul, and imagination dictate. Therefore, it is far better to point out some strengths in *all* products submitted by children than to single out certain ones as "the best." Moreover, pointing out a variety of strong elements in all creative work helps children to begin to evaluate their own work in a nonthreatening way. If a teacher must discuss limitations of creative work, he or she may use samples by anonymous students from past classes to point out an artistic technique or a mode of discourse that failed, in the teacher's opinion, to reach the desired objective. In this way children can begin to assess creative work and the teacher can demonstrate certain deficiencies in it, but no child feels personally responsible for creating an inadequate product.

- *Fend off all negative criticism.* Similarly, if a classroom in which children feel free to take creative risks is desired, those children must be certain that they are safe from hurtful criticism about their creative expressions. Children must be taught how to respond tactfully to the work of others, initially with positive statements of appreciation, and then by questions that might ask for elaboration or clarification from the creator. Using a teacher-made response guide (see this chapter's appendix) that includes a variety of specific positive statements as well as helpful questions that children could ask about a piece of creative work will assist children in learning to react to each other's work diplomatically.

  Additionally, providing practice using the response guides to respond to anonymous creative work will allow children to feel more confident in their ability to offer praise and helpful suggestions.

SUMMARY

One of the main tasks of education should be to foster creative expression, for the symbols of both art and language help children to communicate and make sense of their world. However, the term creativity is too often misinterpreted so that parents and educators feel that a focus on creativity will necessitate a deemphasis on basic skills.

This chapter calls for a more inclusive definition of creativity that will celebrate every possible creative manifestation that a child may offer, covering not only "studio art" products, but products that cut across the entire elementary curriculum.

Specific suggestions were offered for building a classroom climate where creative thinking and expression could best be fostered. In such a climate, basic skills need *not* be deemphasized, but rather a variety of ways to arrive at answers underscored. In a creative climate, literacy and the arts can synergistically blend and flow, and the uniqueness of each individual can be invited forth. Most importantly, through creativity that can be expressed in language and the arts, children can come to terms with their own identities and develop ways to respond to their own perceptions of the world.

QUESTIONS FOR JOURNAL WRITING AND DISCUSSION

1. What is your personal definition of creativity? How will your ideas incorporate all the ways that children might express themselves?

2. What experiences can you recall that you may have had with the Initiation-Response-Evaluation (IRE) technique used by elementary teachers? How did you feel about contributing to such a discussion?

3. Discuss your feelings about the differences between traditional report card grading and portfolio assessment. Which method would be superior for promoting self-motivated learning? Why do you think so?

SUGGESTIONS FOR PROJECTS

1. Plan a replication of the author's "test" of creativity. Ask one friend to consider a box, giving him or her these instructions: "Think of as many things as you can that can be done with this box." To another friend who has not heard the first set of instructions, give these directions: "Think of as many creative, clever things as you can to do with this box. Only write down creative, high-quality ideas." Give each person five minutes to brainstorm. Which person came up with the most ideas? Compare their satisfaction with the experiment.

2. Survey a group of teachers and ask them their definition of creativity. Ask them to explain how their definition impacts their classroom practice.
3. Give a group of children four or five ordinary objects (e.g., a dish towel, a hat, a ball, a plastic flower, a container, etc.). Ask them to create a group story using these objects. What statements could you make about the creativity of the children? How do you think the product might be different if you had used younger children? Older children? Adults?

REFERENCES

Calabria, F. (1977). The why of creative dramatics. *Instructor*, 77, 182–187.

California Department of Education. (1992). *It's elementary!* Elementary Grades Task Force Report. Sacramento: California Department of Education.

Roller, C. (1989). Classroom interaction patterns: Reflections of a stratified society. *Language Arts*, 66(5), 492–500.

Schutz, W. C. (1967). *Joy*. New York: Grove Press.

Scofield, R. W. (1960). A creative climate. *Educational Leadership*, 18, 5–6.

Sternberg, R. J., & Lubart, T. I. (1991). Creating creative minds. *Phi Delta Kappan*, 72, 608–614.

APPENDIX

Response Guide

RESPONSES TO WRITTEN WORK

I like the part where . . .

I'd like to know more about . . .

I liked the order you used in your writing because . . .

I got confused in the part where . . .

You used some powerful words, like . . .

I liked the way you explained . . .

Your writing made me feel . . .

I like the way the character said . . .

The dialogue was realistic when . . .

Could you add more to this part because . . . ?

Could you combine these sentences?

Could you use a different word for . . . ?

Could you write an opening sentence to "grab" the reader?

Do you need a closing?

Could you leave this part out because . . .

Are your paragraphs in the right order?

RESPONSES TO OTHER CREATIVE WORK

This makes me feel . . .

I like the way you used color because . . .

This reminds me of . . .

What was your purpose in creating this work?

What does this work mean to you?

The subject you chose is interesting to me because . . .

How does this work compare to others you have created?

How did you happen to think of your idea for this work?

CHAPTER **4**

Visualization Activities: The Ignition Key

There is probably a good reason for the often heard cliché, "It was a great movie, but the book was even better." Most people who really do enjoy reading use the incredible resource of their own imagination while reading a good book. They actively bring their own myriad of life's experiences to the text, allowing their minds to vividly color the characters and events exactly the way they wish them to be. The text comes alive for them in the most personal and intense kind of way. No wonder the film—always a far cry from what the fertile imagination can conjure—is a disappointment to them!

In today's high-tech world, the old cliché is not heard often among young people. It is possible that we are shortchanging them by taking away the imaginative challenges in their recreational activities. Instead of children making up a fanciful dialogue with their teddy bears, for example, such toys can now instigate and control sophisticated "conversations," while video games have become so vividly graphic that virtually nothing needs to be imagined. Even popular songs now provide lavishly produced videos, dismissing the need for youngsters to call up any of their own images to make the lyrics come alive.

THE IMPORTANCE OF VISUALIZATION

Because children are being given fewer and fewer opportunities to use their imaginations naturally, it becomes crucial to include visualization activities in a program that integrates literacy and the arts. For one thing, when children are in the midst of the creative process, they must be able to consult their own personal "mind pictures"—their own collection of learnings, experiences, emotions, and impressions—to decide what should come next in their work. Visualization exercises can strengthen this ability, making it almost second nature for children. As a result, they become more confident and capable when attempting to creatively express themselves.

Additionally, encouraging children to actively visualize words and concepts may not only help them to enjoy reading more, but it can also improve their understanding of what they read (Long, Winograd, & Bridge, 1989; Oliver, 1982; Pressley, 1976). One program implemented in California is a case in point: Children were taught to recognize key words and then develop mental images from them. They then did oral reading exercises to verify these images. The result of this program was comprehension gains significantly above those of previous years (Escondido Union School District, 1979).

Visualization activities that can be used as motivational prewriting prompts will also help children to derive more pleasure from reading as they use their imagination to appreciate sensory and descriptive imagery. Teachers can also familiarize their students with the metacognitive strategy of turning to their own personal mind pictures for guidance when reading, writing, or participating in other creative expressions.

Guidelines for Using Visualization

The abilities to conceptualize and to use language have a kind of symbiotic relationship; that is, ability or practice in one tends to reinforce the other, culminating in enhanced learning. Through the experience of frequent language use, the quality of thoughts can be improved; similarly, by enriching thoughts and the quality and quantity of mental images, language facility can be heightened. Through imaging exercises that are followed by speaking, drawing, and writing activities, a child's transitory thoughts can be transformed into concrete ideas that can be shared with others. This transformation happens when single ideas merge with prior ideas a child holds on the same topic. This collection of ideas is then stored in a theoretical structure researchers call *schema* (Block, 1993). Each schema the child holds is actually the sum total of all the impressions, associations, experiences, and emotions that that child has about the topic. Therefore, any visualization or imaging activity that a teacher guides children through will necessarily result in a wide variety of images about any topic because the responses totally depend upon the schema of each individual child and just how fully each child's schema has been activated, or brought to the conscious mind, by the stimulus.

To obtain the optimal language benefits from the routine use of visualization, the sensitive teacher may want to keep in mind the following general guidelines to help activate the particular schema of each child (Fredericks, 1986):

1. Children first need to be reassured that there are no "correct" or "incorrect" mind pictures; whatever their imaginations dictate are valid responses. Children must feel safe to speak freely about what they envision.
2. Children must learn to respect each other's mind pictures, understanding that the images that pop into one's mind are often influenced by one's

own past experiences, learnings, or emotions—in other words, by their own schema.

3. Children need enough "wait time" to bring forth their images. If they are rushed, some children will draw blanks and begin to believe that their imaginations are somehow inadequate.
4. Teachers must allow sufficient time to discuss images in a supportive, cooperative, and informal atmosphere that conveys to children the feeling that everyone's images are worth exploring.
5. Parents and teachers need to help children to develop the skill of language elaboration by actively seeking details about their contributions. For example, if a child offers, "I see a blue horse," the teacher might reply, "Oh—that's interesting! Tell us more about the blue horse."

TEACHING CHILDREN TO VISUALIZE

For some language-fluent children, visualization comes quite easily, and they write prolifically without interruption. Others may need practice creating images in their minds as a precursor to writing. As Gardner and Hatch (1989) have observed: "The relationship between language and thinking has been a topic of debate for a very long time. However, nearly every program we have considered acknowledges the importance of language facility to effective thinking in one way or another." (p. 48)

D. D. Mundell (1985) has presented a four-step process for helping children to more actively use their imaginations:

1. Give children practice visualizing concrete objects. Such an activity helps children to focus their attention on a particular array of visual details.
2. Give children practice recalling scenes or experiences from outside the classroom. Children then begin to understand that their repertoire of impressions are "on tap," to be called upon at will.
3. Give children practice listening to high-imagery stories and relating them to their own experiences. Such practice helps children to incorporate new information with their established collection of impressions to form a new, enriched schema.
4. Teach children to trust their mind pictures to tell them what could happen next in their oral and written creations. As children become more adept at activating their own schema, they begin to benefit from the tremendous power of their own minds. New language and ideas are always available about any topic with which they are familiar.

IDEAS FOR CLASSROOM PRACTICE

The following examples show how Mundell's four-step process could be implemented in an elementary classroom.

Give Children Practice Visualizing Objects

Allow children the opportunity to look very carefully at everyday objects, such as the pencil sharpener, a favorite toy, or their tennis shoes. Have them close their eyes and try to recreate every detail of the object in their minds, and then with their eyes open, compare their mental image with the actual object. Finally, let them verbally or pictorially try to create the object, attempting to include even those details they had overlooked the first time.

For an added oral language dimension to the previous exercise, have one child select an object and put it in a bag so that it is out of sight to the other members of the class. Let the child describe all the visual attributes of the object that would help the other children identify it while the others try to draw the object from the child's description. Then compare the object with the children's drawings and discuss the reasons for the sometimes humorous discrepancies between the drawings and the actual object.

As a variation of this activity, select a child to leave the classroom for a few moments. Have the rest of the children in the class describe or draw the absent child by trying to visualize everything that individual was wearing, plus the person's height, weight, and color of eyes and hair. When the child reenters the classroom, compare the class members' visual memories with the child's actual appearance.

Give Children Practice Recalling Scenes or Experiences from Outside the Classroom

To help children become more accurate observers, ask them to close their eyes and picture their family car (or pet, or living room). As they are thinking about it, orally "walk" them around the outside of the car, telling them to try and imagine the wheels, the hubcaps, the doors (two or four?), the color of the paint, the grille, the license plates, and so on. Next, have the children draw a picture of the car with as much detail as they can remember. Then ask them to take their drawings home and compare them with the actual vehicles.

Every child has watched a helium-filled balloon go up into the sky until it is out of sight. Key into this experience, common to children, by showing them the film *The Red Balloon.* Then follow the viewing by reading aloud Shel Silverstein's poem "Eight Balloons," while the children close their eyes. (This poem describes the journey of eight balloons whose sad fates range from landing on a frying pan to entering a crocodile's mouth.) Ask the children to imagine they are holding their own helium-filled balloons, which suddenly escape into the air. Give them a few moments to imagine the flight of their balloons and then encourage them to give an oral or pictorial account of one balloon's journey.

Demonstrate to children how their visual and olfactory senses combine to create even stronger memories. Let them smell several items with strong aromas without revealing to the children what they are. Have children close their eyes and sniff items whose odors usually evoke explicit memories of past experiences, such as leather, pine cones, a plastic doll, bubble gum, or lavender sachet. Ask children to share the mental images that come to their minds about people and places that they associate with these scents.

Give Children Practice Listening to High Imagery Stories and Relating Them to Their Own Experiences

Read aloud stories that contain a great deal of visual imagery, such as the books *Tuck Everlasting* or *Julie of the Wolves*. Stop every so often and allow children to share their mental images of how the characters, settings, or events have come to life in their minds.

Also do "mental adventure" exercises on a routine basis. Ask the children to close their eyes and orally give them guided imagery of a situation, such as a safari in deepest Africa, or a tamer adventure, like a walk through a nearby wooded area. For example:

"Picture yourself in a forest. You are strolling among the trees on a well-worn path. What is the weather like? [*Pause to let children imagine.*] As you walk along, you see a person. You exchange glances with the person, and then that person runs quickly in the other direction. Why? [*Pause.*] You continue walking and soon come to a body of water. What is it? How deep, how wide, how cold? [*Pause.*] You cross it. How? [*Pause.*] You find the path again on the other side and begin walking. Soon you almost trip on a cup lying in the middle of the path. You stoop to pick it up and examine it carefully. What does it look like? [*Pause.*] You put it down. Why? [*Pause.*] You keep walking until the path leads to a fence. You climb over the fence and see a house. What does the house look like? [*Pause.*] You enter the house and find yourself in the kitchen. What is the kitchen like? [*Pause.*] You sit at the kitchen table and see that there is something interesting on the table. What is it? [*Pause.*] While you are looking at it, the person whom you saw in the forest walks into the kitchen. Describe that person."

Ask the children then to orally retrace their individual journeys for the class, or, at later stages, to do it in written form.

Allow pairs of children to act out their journeys for the rest of the class, if they wish, or to draw their journey sequentially.

Another high-imagery listening experience that you can provide for your class is to have them listen to *The Adventures of Robinson Crusoe* (Defoe, 1991), *The Cay* (Taylor, 1969), or *Swiss Family Robinson* (Wyss, 1991). Have them close their eyes and visualize their own versions of a shipwreck. Then, over the period of time during which the story is read, ask them to write a series of journal entries of their adventures on their own make-believe islands, encouraging them to "borrow" as much as they would like from the text. Let each child select his or her own favorite entry to dramatize into an original one-act play that can be performed for the rest of the class.

Teach Children to Trust Their Mind Pictures to Tell Them What Could Happen Next in Their Oral and Written Creations

To provide the children with the "ignition key" that will always be at their disposal when they are writing independently, Spontaneous Story Technique (SST) (Kolpakoff, 1986) can serve as the bridge to link together a child's pictorial imagination, oral language, and writing. This method is ideal at all grade levels, but requires much practice and the initial enthusiastic participation of the teacher as storyteller.

To begin using this technique, children should be gathered around the teacher in a relaxed fashion, preferably on the floor. Then the teacher instructs the students to close their eyes and make their minds as empty as possible. The rest of a typical SST exercise goes something like this:

"Now your mind is empty. But as soon as you 'see' something, raise your hand." The teacher then solicits responses that individual children have visualized and encourages their elaboration.

"Again, I want you to make your mind as empty as possible, but this time I'm going to ask you to do something very strange. When I tell you *not* to see something, try as hard as you can, *not* to see it. Now—*do not* see a pink giraffe!"

Stop and discuss with the children how many of them actually did see a pink giraffe, and have children share what their various giraffes looked like. Continue in this manner with several other examples of things you tell children *not* to see.

"Now I want you to make your mind empty once more and hold it empty for as long as you can. When a picture does come into your mind, raise your hand." Wait until all hands are raised and then encourage the children to describe their mental images. Praise effective elaboration that allows other children to "see" too.

"I am now going to ask you to put your last picture back in your mind. Hold that picture there as long as you can. When that picture goes away or changes to a new picture, please raise your hand." Let the children orally share their pictures.

After a number of SST sessions, when children have become much more confident about using their imaginations and willingly sharing their images, they are ready to begin using these visual skills to develop endings to stories. They can now be assured that they can always know what comes next in a story; all they have to do is to allow their minds to create the next picture. At this stage, the teacher will want to tell a cliffhanger story. In later sessions a story can be told by student volunteers. A cliffhanger story might go like this:

"Close your eyes and let your mind be empty. Now I want you to picture yourself entering a room in an old attic. It is raining and you can hear the soft patter of raindrops on the roof. Hear them? [*Pause.*] You wander around the stuffy attic and notice an old rocking horse and a stuffed rabbit with an ear missing. You walk toward a broken window and see a large spider web. The spider suddenly swoops down to look at you [*pause for squeals from the squeamish*], and then scurries quickly away. Your eye catches a large mirror on the far wall of the attic. It has fancy gold decorations on all sides and is covered with several layers of dust. You move over to it and start to brush off the dust when you discover, to your surprise, that you can walk through the mirror. You push your body through the mirror and you see . . ." At this crucial point, ask children to open their eyes and share their visions of what was on the other side of the mirror.

Other visualization stories could be expanded and used in a similar way:

- "You are exploring a deep, dark cave. You suddenly hear a strong, frightening voice. You try to find your way back to the entrance, but it seems that all the rooms in the cave look very much alike. You panic as you realize the voice is coming closer and closer. Suddenly, you see it is . . . ."

- "You are flying an airplane over some corn fields in Iowa. Suddenly the engine starts to sputter and the plane begins to lose altitude. You quickly put on your parachute. You are as scared as you have ever been, but you jump out of the plane, and . . . ."
- "You are skindiving off the coast of Australia. You are having fun playing hide and seek with the groupers and friendly parrot fish. Suddenly you spy an old abandoned ship and you dive down to explore it. You open the door to the captain's quarters and are amazed to find that. . . ." (Cecil, 1989, p.101)

When the children are feeling confident that they can anticipate what will happen next in a story through their mind pictures, they are ready to begin using storyboards to help them finish their stories. The storyboard for primary-age children is a piece of paper divided into panels on which children pictorially sequence the next events in the story. For older children, the panels are the next six pages of text; for younger children, use fewer panels.

Individual tape recorders are sometimes useful to help children make the transition from mind pictures to the oral telling of incidents and then to the written version. With the tape recorder, the children can revise and expand their text until they are completely satisfied with their story before writing anything. Then they can use their recording to help them transcribe the narrative onto paper, continually checking with their mind pictures for any new information.

While the children are busy writing, the teacher's role is to interact with the students in a nondirective way to help them with their writing problems and temporary blocks. Ivan Kolpakoff (1986) suggests three specific interactive techniques that can enable the teacher to become a more effective writing facilitator:

1. *Marking time*. When children tell the teacher that they don't know what comes next, the teacher may deliberately *not* respond to this lament and, instead, distract the child from the writing task by instigating a very brief chat about something totally unrelated to the child's current writing. This chance for the child to get away for a few seconds from the intensity of creating often allows that child to return to writing with fresh ideas and an immediate inspiration. This ploy is used often by professional writers.
2. *Next picture*. When a child is "stuck," another technique is to read the child's work and then suggest a thought that could lead to new ideas. For example, a child writing about the mirror in the attic may be blocked when he or she sees a picnic area on the other side of the mirror but can't get an idea of what happens there. The teacher might suggest, "I see a little boy running away from his parents into the woods and . . . " At that point the teacher smiles and walks away, promising to check back later to see how the author is doing. Jack Canfield and Frank

Siccone (1993) suggest that when children become stuck or blocked, teachers invite them to contact "central control" for guidance in solving the problem. The fictional central control can send them a magic wand, a power booster, a guru, or whatever might lead them to the solutions that are, after all, right in their own imaginations.

3. *Writer's talk.* Because the teacher is ordinarily so engrossed in the role of support person, too often the only real intellectual exchange between the teacher and young author is to offer help or to answer a request for assistance. Another important role for the teacher when children are writing their imaginative ideas is to talk to each child, author to author, making respectful comments about each other's imaginative thoughts and ideas. Teachers are then able to be perceived as helpful collaborators rather than powerful beings with all the answers.

VISUALIZATION ACROSS THE CURRICULUM

In one elementary classroom in Sacramento, California, the school day begins with visualization so that the children may mentally prepare themselves for the academic activities of the day. Soft music is played and the lights are dimmed as the children relax and create visual images from the teacher's guided imagery script that describes upcoming lessons. After the imagery, each child is invited to share his or her images with the rest of the class.

Visualization is also utilized as a tool for classroom management and conflict resolution in this class. Before any hands-on activity or group work at their desks, the children may image themselves following very specific instructions, and see themselves engaging in the activity that the teacher has described to them. When it is time for the children to return to their desks, they have imagined themselves beginning to use appropriate social behavior. Before recess, the children are often asked to visualize themselves sharing the jumprope, taking turns on the playground equipment, or walking quietly back to the classroom when it is time to come in. After recess, the teacher sometimes uses visualization to help the children to re-create a conflict that just occurred on the playground and to think about some alternative solutions to its resolution. The visualization then leads to oral discussion and journal writing (Sommer, 1990).

The skill of visualizing should have a prominent place in many areas of a whole-language elementary curriculum, where the language arts are thoroughly integrated, especially when abstract concepts and ideas need to be made more concrete and meaningful for younger children. Social studies, for example, requires children to do much writing of an analytical/expository nature; and when guided imagery is used, children can become more personally involved through the sensory/descriptive information that visualization provides for them.

Dale Sprowl (1986) uses the image of present, familiar situations to help children relate to difficult and abstract concepts. For example, to show children how technology has affected their lives, he asks them to close their eyes and imagine that it is early morning and they are in the bathroom trying to get ready for school. He then asks them to mentally take away any machines that they would normally use, such as electric toothbrushes, hair dryers, or electric rollers. Of course, there is no light in the bathroom. Next, he has them picture themselves walking to their bedroom, erasing the images of their radio or stereo, or even any clothing that was made by machine. On the way to the kitchen they pass through the living room, which is now bereft of the telephone, television, VCR, and again, lights. The children must then try to imagine their kitchen without the stove, refrigerator, washer, dryer, or dishwasher. Finally, he instructs the children to do away with even the walls and the carpets, as these items, too, are made by machines.

Because this mental voyage is so graphic and personal for children, they truly begin to understand, in a very memorable way, the concept of a world without the modern technology that they quite naturally take for granted. Such guided imagery can also be used to effectively introduce other important global concepts, such as poverty, racism, nuclear war, or life in another country, to name just a few.

SUMMARY

Visualization activities invest children with the ability to look inside themselves to "see" stories more clearly and to trust that their own minds will know what should happen next in their own creations. The skill is a fundamental technique that should be at the core of any program that purports to integrate literacy and the arts, for it quite clearly demonstrates to children that they must be active, rather than passive, participants in their own development as writers, readers, and creative thinkers. Visualization gives them a tool to communicate more effectively. It is a tool that almost all children possess, but somehow, somewhere, it is often discarded in deference to other external demands placed upon them. By using visualization activities and their fertile imaginations in their writing, reading, and creative expression, children will be delighted to find that a whole army of wonderful ideas is very much alive somewhere in their minds, patiently waiting to be invited onto the page.

QUESTIONS FOR JOURNAL WRITING AND DISCUSSION

1. React to the statement "It was a great movie but the book was even better." Have you ever experienced this? Describe the book you chose and how you imagined the characters in your own way.
2. Have you ever experienced "writer's block"? What did you do to resume the writing process? How might the technique of visualizing "the next picture" have helped in this situation?
3. Using the technique of visualization, close your eyes and think about your last vacation. What pictures came to your mind? Conceptualize them in oral form for discussion or in written form for journal writing.

SUGGESTIONS FOR PROJECTS

1. Close your eyes and picture your living room or your car. Try to visualize every detail of the room or car, touching every part of it and imagining the colors, the textures, and so on. Draw a picture of the car or room and compare it to the "real thing." What was lacking? What did you learn from this experience that will help you to assist young children with their visualizing experiences?

2. Observe a child as he or she conducts a dialogue with a simple rag doll. Observe the same child playing with a more sophisticated doll that talks or performs other natural functions. What do you see as the difference in the quality of the play?

3. Survey a group of elementary-age youngsters to determine if they are more apt to read a book if they have seen the movie, or if they are more apt to want to see a movie if they have read the book. What reasons did they give for their choices?

REFERENCES

Block, C. C. (1993). *Teaching the language arts: Expanding thinking through student-centered instruction.* Boston: Allyn & Bacon.

Canfield, J., & Siccone, F. (1993). *101 ways to develop student self-esteem and responsibility, volume 1: The teacher as coach.* Boston: Allyn & Bacon.

Cecil, N. L. (1989). *Freedom fighters: Affective teaching of the language arts.* Salem, WI: Sheffield.

Defoe, D. (1991). *The adventures of Robinson Crusoe.* White Plains, NY: Longman.

Escondido Union School District. (1979). *Mind's eyes: Creating mental pictures from printed words.* Escondido, CA: Escondido School District Board of Education.

Fredericks, A. (1986). Mental imagery activities to improve comprehension. *The Reading Teacher, 40,* 78–71.

Gardner, H., & Hatch, T. (1989). Multiple intelligences go to school: Educational implications of the theory of multiple intelligences. *Educational Researcher, 18* (8), 4–10.

Kolpakoff, I. (1986). *Spontaneous story technique.* Unpublished manuscript.

Long, S., Winograd, P., & Bridge, C. (1989). The effects of reader and text characteristics on imagery reported during and after reading. *Reading Research Quarterly, 24,* 359–371.

Mundell, D. D. (1985). *Mental imagery: Do you see what I see?* Oklahoma City: Oklahoma State Department of Education.

Oliver, M. E. (1982). *Improving comprehension with mental imagery.* ERIC Document Reproduction Service No. ED220818.

Pressley, G. M. (1976). Mental imagery helps eight-year-olds remember what they read. *Journal of Educational Psychology, 68,* 355–359.

Sommer, S. B. (1990). Putting the pieces back together: Integrating the language arts. In N. L. Cecil (Ed.), *Literacy in the '90s: Readings in the language arts* (pp. 198–207). Dubuque, IA: Kendall/Hunt.

Sprowl, D. (1986). Guided imagery in the social studies. In *Practical ideas for teaching writing as a process.* Sacramento: California State Department of Education.

Taylor, T. (1969). *The cay.* New York: Avon.

Wyss, J. (1991). *Swiss family Robinson.* New York: Scholastic.

PART II

Expression: Curriculum Experiences in the Arts

CHAPTER 5

Art and Children's Literature: The Vision

Integrating art and children's literature is nothing new. Many teachers earnestly avow that they have, for years, been following the reading aloud of a story with some vaguely related art activity: The teacher reads Ezra Jack Keats's *The Snowy Day* to the first-grade class, for example, and then shows the children how to create snowflakes by folding and cutting white construction paper. Thirty nearly identical snowflakes soon line the periphery of the classroom. The teacher has integrated art and literature—or has this occurred? While children have engaged in two enjoyable, yet discrete, communication activities, it seems doubtful that the snowflake-making session has added anything significant to the appreciation of Keats's delicate text, nor has much been added to the children's understanding of themselves as artists.

Similarly, with the proliferation of the studies currently exploring emergent literacy (Morrow, Burks, & Rand, 1992), primary teachers now know that it is sound educational practice to allow children to draw a picture and then dictate a story to accompany their magnum opus. Or, sometimes, children write their own story using invented spelling to go along with their picture. Is this, then, the true integration of drawing and language arts? It certainly offers children an opportunity to become aware of and experiment with various artistic tensions. Yet sometimes, some of the children's spontaneous dialogue becomes lost. The sole illustration for the story is only a "slide," and thus inspires a disappointingly stilted phrase from a child, when what that child actually had in mind was a vivacious, multiframed video (Dyson, 1986). As in the previous illustration, both art and story are compromised.

At the very heart of the integration of art and literature is the artist and his or her "vision": the angst and the burning desire to create; the search for a solution to a creative puzzle that will at once assuage and delight the senses—*this* is the content of literature that can be most successfully harmonized with art.

As a personal example, I have just finished reading a novel by Anne Tyler titled *Celestial Navigation* (1984). One of the main characters in this book is an artist named Jeremy. The author provides a sensitive portrayal of Jeremy's total fascination with color, texture, and the planes in faces as he goes about creating his sculptures. These vivid descriptions fill me with great awe and wonderment. My ultimate reaction—and that of those colleagues with whom I have had the opportunity of discussing the book—is one of a new openness and appreciation of the creation of a piece of sculpture, plus a real desire to try my own hand at it. I feel eager to share Jeremy's intensity about his work, and I am convinced that, through literature, children can share this eagerness, too.

The bibliography of children's literature in the appendix provides a host of children's literature that also contains characters for whom art, music, or poetry is a significant facet of their lives. The remainder of this chapter looks at four samples of such literature and explores how it can help children to understand an artist's vision—how an artist thinks about art and life. The chapter also discusses how such literature often provides a natural segue into art activities that, instead of being frivolous additions, significantly increase the understanding of the text, or provide what reader-responses theorists term *literacy evocation* (Cox & Many, 1992). Finally, the chapter offers suggestions as to how children's artistic creations, inspired by children's literature, can be celebrated and shared with the community.

PICTURE STORYBOOKS ABOUT ARTISTS

Tomie dePaola's *The Art Lesson* (1989) and Cynthia Rylant's *All I See* (1988) are two picture storybooks whose major characters see the world in a special way and are obsessed with sharing their vision on paper. In *The Art Lesson*, Tommy likes to draw more than anything else in the world. While "Jack collected all kinds of turtles . . . Herbie made huge cities in his sandbox . . . and Jeannie, Tommy's best friend, did cartwheels and stood on her head . . . Tommy drew and drew and drew" (pp. 3, 4). His grown-up cousins are in college, studying to be artists, and they give Tommy two pieces of advice: practice continually and don't copy! But when Tommy finally gets to have art lessons in first grade, the first thing his art teacher does is to draw a picture of a Pilgrim on the chalkboard and exhort all the children to "watch carefully and copy me." Since this instruction goes against everything Tommy's cousins—and his artist's instinct—tell him he should do, he quietly protests. A compromise is reached when the art teacher suggests that Tommy draw the Pilgrim the teacher's way, and then draw his own picture of the Pilgrim as he sees it. Tommy agrees, and the remaining pages are filled with the child's rich idiosyncratic drawings of the world he sees around him.

One second-grade teacher followed the reading of *The Art Lesson* by telling the class the story of *The Blind Man and the Elephant*. The children then discussed how it is possible to see things in many different ways with each person being "right," just as Tommy did and other artists do. The teacher then asked the children to look around the room and select something, or someone, they wished to draw, as Tommy did in the story. They were gently reminded *not* to copy one another, as Tommy's cousins had advised him. The session ended with the children sharing their unique drawings with the class. Several children remarked, in their own words, that they felt much "freer" to draw in their own way because they knew their piece would be original and thus not open to comparison with any other piece in the class.

In *All I See*, Cynthia Rylant has created a story about two people, one a young man and the other a little boy, who are drawn together by their love of painting. Every morning the boy, Charlie, watches surreptitiously as the artist, Gregory, goes down to the edge of a lake and paints pictures of blue whales. Each day, after Gregory leaves, Charlie sneaks over to the canvas to take a look at the latest rendering of a blue whale. One day Charlie finds no whale—only a blank canvas. Using Gregory's paints, Charlie paints his own picture of Gregory gaily painting and humming by the lake. The next day, when Charlie pads down to the shore of the lake to see what Gregory has painted, he sees only a sign written in paint: I LIKED YOUR PICTURE. Several days later, Charlie overcomes his shyness enough to come out of hiding and watch Gregory paint. Gregory instantly befriends the little boy. He teaches him "about shadow and light, about line, about drawing things near and things far away . . ." (p. 21). Gregory buys Charlie an easel, paints, and several new brushes and delights in watching him paint. Finally, Charlie summons up the courage to ask Gregory the question that has long been on his mind: Why does he only paint pictures of blue whales? Gregory smiles and thinks for a moment, and then replies, "It is all I see." Charlie has *never* seen a whale in the lake, but he begins to understand that "seeing" means something very special to an artist.

Such a luminous story can be used to underscore a very important idea in art: what one sees is not always seen with one's eyes. Indeed, many artists do not paint what is before them at all, but rather dredge up remembered people, places, and feelings and then color either their interpretations of them with their own affective filters, or sometimes, what they wish they might find.

The teacher can use guided imagery to encourage children to use their mind's eye to visualize—in reality or using "wish fulfillment"—their own homes. The teacher can facilitate the process by taking the children on a pretend "walking tour" through their homes, inviting the children to evoke feelings, memories, aromas, textures of furniture, colors, brightness, mood, and so on. Then, providing colored pencils, crayons, or colored chalk, the teacher can encourage the children to sketch their impressions in an attempt to evoke as many of their memories as possible.

In a follow-up session, children are usually ready and eager to move from the familiar to the unfamiliar with their artistic impressions. Using verbal cues similar to those given in the previous activity, the teacher can bring children to the edge of the lake by which Charlie and Gregory painted. Providing painting materials, the teacher can then invite children to "paint all they see." The activity brings children to new levels of aesthetic sensitivity and offers a high regard for each child's own artistic vision.

BOOKS ABOUT ARTISTS FOR YOUNG ADULTS

Zibby Oneal's *In Summer Light* (1986) and Colby Rodowsky's *Julie's Daughter* (1985) both have as major characters artists for whom creative expression is a driving force in their lives. They also portray appealing youngsters who are experiencing the pain of growing up and finding their own identities. Much as reading instruction uses a "think aloud" strategy to model how critical meaning is gleaned, these novels model, through their characters' musings, the struggles with creative problem solving and artistic judgments that artists go through when working their craft.

Julie's Daughter concerns a mother, Julie, and her daughter, Slug, whom Julie left behind when the child was 3 years old. Harper Tegges is an independent, elderly artist who brings mother and daughter together through their concern for her. The story begins with Julie returning home for her mother's funeral. There she encounters Slug, who has been living with her grandmother for the past 17 years. On impulse, Julie offers to take Slug home to live with her. This is the moment that Slug has been dreaming of her entire life; however, the reality is not as wonderful as the fantasy. Julie is virtually a stranger to Slug, and the two are uncomfortable with one another. Mother and daughter begin to go their separate ways. Then, Harper Tegges becomes very ill and, as both mother and daughter care for her and mourn her impending death, the two begin to confront the resentments of their past and learn to reach out to one another.

In this novel, the voices of Julie, Slug, and Harper Tegges are interwoven throughout the story. It is in the chapters about Harper that the intensity of the artist's vision becomes clear. When Harper becomes ill and falls down, her first thought is whether her right hand, her "good friend" that enables her to paint, is still intact. Later, when her neighbors help her up and into her bedroom, she is concerned that they will see the rough sketches she has drawn for a planned painting of the neighborhood. The neighbors do notice the sketches, but as Harper so insightfully observes, they haven't really "seen" them at all:

> But the houses were there. My big back doors. Roof tops. Porch spindles. Steps. And bits of people too. The mailman in an elongated letter shaped like a kite. The pattern of Mrs. Bigelow's zinnias. Abstracts of Mattie Miller's dogs. David's car in pieces on the sidewalk. Marion's washing hung all in a row. Ernestus Stokes seen as a metronome. And Julie as a bird. A suggestion of the stream bed was there, too, and the hill, going up and down. (p. 13)

Here the reader again gains access into the mind of a unique artistic vision. Unlike the neighbors, Harper Tegges sees her community as a fascinating mosaic of patterns and details. She also reveals a delightful habit of summarizing people metaphorically—Julie as a "bird" and Ernestus Stokes as a "metronome."

Such vision has the capacity to stimulate young readers and to make them eager to reflect upon how *they* see people and the world. After reading this book one sixth-grade class, of their own accord, spent their entire recess sketching other children on the playground and jotting down some metaphors that their movements brought to mind. Later, the children enthusiastically shared their sketches with their classmates, struggling to articulate exactly what it was the children did that inspired their sketches and their particular choices of comparison with other things.

In a different segment of *Julie's Daughter*, the author allows the reader to eavesdrop on Harper's stream of consciousness as she creates. Suddenly painting can be seen as a most demanding pursuit, much like an arduous competition between the artist's hand, eye, and the inner recesses of her soul that combine, in the end, to form a triumphant entity. Harper shares how, when her act of creation is going well, the piece takes on a will of its own:

> Stepping back, I held my hand out from my forehead to bring it back into perspective, to see on the canvas what I had seen before. Then I took up a piece of charcoal and began laying in figures and shapes. The suggestion of a girl was there again, and this time I let her stay. I worked frantically, feverishly, until it was as if the studio couldn't contain me anymore. And I was through the wide-open doors and out onto the grass, swaying at first, then dancing. . . . The painting drove me. Demanded things of me. And the work was drudging and unsparing. (pp. 27–34)

Again such a passage allows the reader to enter into the mind of the artist and vicariously experience the frustration—as well as the thrill—of executing a totally absorbing artistic creation. After reading this particular section, one sports-minded young boy admitted that it had caused him to acquire a new respect for art; he offered that he would now be much more open to trying his own hand at painting. In a class discussion, the boy shared his observation that painting, as described by

Harper Tegges, "sounds a lot like running, when I sometimes lose control of my feet and just go with them wherever they take me." He admitted that he now felt that painting was not merely "girl stuff" after all, but a vigorous and worthwhile pastime (Stover, 1988).

Kate, the main character in Oneal's *In Summer Light* (1986), is physically and emotionally running away from being compared with her father, Marcus, a well-known artist. Kate chooses to go to boarding school to escape her judgmental and domineering parent, but an illness forces her to return home to recuperate. Kate befriends Ian, a handsome young student who has been hired by Kate's father to be his assistant. Ian encourages Kate to come to terms with her own artistic ability, which has been dormant for many years, due, in part, to her unwillingness to be compared with her famous father. Ian gently guides Kate to return to the unrestrictive kind of expressive art she had loved as a little child: rock painting, in which she created swirls and bold pictures on boulders with handfuls of red clay "paint." The author's descriptions of Kate's thoughts while she paints rocks allow the reader to feel her utter joy as she becomes totally immersed in the activity:

> She made a series of curves, scooping clay and sweeping it higher on the rock, using the palms of her hands and her fingers like brushes. Water lapped at her ankles, and the red clay ran down her arms, streaking her with red. She scooped and painted, laying great overlapping strokes, interlocking curves, spiraling patterns. She did a series of snail whorls that she remembered seeing on a Cretan vase. Then a sort of free-form octopus shape. Shapes and patterns came to her from pictures she'd looked at, from pottery she'd seen in glass cases in echoing museum rooms. She forgot to look at Ian. She began not to hear the voices of the children on the beach. (p. 53)

Kate learns to realize her own artistic gift, which is different from her father's and different still from her mother's, who also used to paint. Kate sees that her mother can draw an adequate figure, and that her father is most interested in how color fills space. All these artists' visions differ. But by the end of the novel, Kate and her father have discovered their piece of bonding commonality: they are both compelled to paint.

The children in one sixth-grade class who had read this novel were quite taken with the scenes of Kate painting in gleeful abandon on the rocks by the beach. While the class had no immediate access to similar cliffs and red clay, the teacher keyed in instead on the two concepts of "going back to an earlier time" and "youthful abandon." The teacher then invited students to finger-paint as they had in kindergarten. Because of their intense identification with Kate's rock painting spree, these sixth-grade children, who generally considered themselves quite "sophisticated," not only enthusiastically participated in the finger painting by making "spiral patterns" and "snail whorls," but were also able to express their own wistfulness for a time gone by when they could create without self-censoring and without immediate concern for the aesthetic reception their products might receive from others.

In each of the four books previously discussed, the theme is that of an artist's struggle to put his or her vision down on paper or canvas. But a further value of these characters from children's literature, as well as of those listed in the bibliography, is that they are deftly created to be realistic, multidimensional human beings with whom children can readily identify and for whom they can come to care about. Thus, such characters inspire children to create, and talk about their creations, in a way that ordinary classroom teachers often cannot.

CELEBRATING THE ARTIST'S CREATION

Artists in children's literature are often portrayed as reaping a kind of internal reward from working on their creations. Most teachers would certainly desire a similar inner motivation for their students to create. However, it is realistic to acknowledge that most children—and adults as well—crave a modicum of external praise and positive feedback for their efforts. Indeed, although most professional artists are internally motivated initially, they, too, thrill to the applause and rave reviews of their public.

Unfortunately, most artwork created by children in the public schools ends up, at best, on the refrigerator door in their homes, for the sole purpose of parental admiration. To give children's artwork the same respect and status merited by the works of fictional artists, a true celebration is in order. Moreover, when a child's own creations are organized for presentation to an audience, those creations suddenly become finally finished in the child's mind and the learning process is complete (Szekely, 1988). Additionally, several of the child's favorite pieces gathered into his or her own display provide a unique opportunity for communicating with other viewers about the works.

IDEAS FOR CLASSROOM PRACTICE

When preparing their students' creations for an art exhibition, the following guidelines may be helpful for teachers (Szekely, 1988):

1. The teacher helps the artists to select their favorite works for display. The pieces may be matted or framed, according to the nature of the pieces and the children's wishes.
2. Various arrangements are experimented with by the artists to determine where, in each artist's viewpoint, the pieces look best. Details such as floor and wall space, as well as the eye level of possible audience members, must also be taken into consideration.
3. The artists make brochures or handouts of their works to describe them or provide additional information about themselves and the genesis of their works. Such data as when and where each piece was created, the inspiration for certain pieces, or interesting facts about how the material

was gathered are among the ideas that might be included in the brochure. Polaroid pictures of the works might also be used for the brochure or for an advance newspaper press kit. A tape recording of suitable music may also be chosen by each artist to enhance the "mood" of the showings.

4. Invitations with the logo or theme of the selected artworks may be designed by the artists and sent to potential guests from the school and/or the community.

5. Optionally, light refreshments could be served to attendees. The choice—including the color, texture, shape, and presentation of the food—can be related to the artist's theme; food for each display may be prepared in advance by the artists.

6. During the actual exhibition, artists can be encouraged to actively interact, involve, and effectively communicate with their public. Before the exhibition, the artists must decide how they would like their guests to respond to their works, and then they can provide oral (on tape or "live") or written instructions for the guests. For example, viewers may be asked to summarize what they are seeing via tracing, redrawing, or by using Etch-a-Sketch materials. In other cases, the audience might be asked to consider the artist's creations while standing on their heads, spinning around, or while using various props, such as colored glasses, binoculars, or a kaleidoscope.

Prior to the exhibition, the teacher's primary roles are that of facilitator and publicist. The teacher should affirm efforts and assist with the practicality of the showing while allowing the artists free creative reign. Additionally, the teacher can be constantly on the lookout for opportunities to move the students' exhibitions out of the school environment and into the larger community so that the artists may encounter fresh perspectives on their work. Malls, hospitals, banks, and even wooden barricades and empty storefronts can serve as wonderful art arenas to provide enthusiastic viewers for children's art.

Each time children's work is exhibited, it is a celebration—a professional recognition of each child's artistic efforts and achievements, and a chance for each artist to communicate his or her ideas with the public. It is also an opportunity for children to share their unique artistic visions with the world and, like the fictional artists they have come to know, to truly begin to respect *themselves* as artists.

SUMMARY

Frequently, integrating art and literature has meant little more than following the reading of any picture storybook with an art activity that is somewhat related to the text. Often, neither the development of literacy nor any significant new artistic understandings has been enhanced with this approach. The teacher has simply attempted to "kill two birds with one stone."

In this chapter, four examples of children's literature have been presented in which a major character is an artist or is in some way impassioned about art. Through the literature itself—by readily identifying with the lifelike characters—children become more open to the various art forms presented and begin to experience, albeit vicariously, the creative compulsion of real-life artists. The characters themselves give children a yearning to create and discover the same intensity that the fictional artists have felt.

This chapter has offered four examples of creative expression directly related to the fictional characters' visions. Teachers are encouraged to use the bibliography in the appendix to find many more selections of children's literature in which art (as well as music, poetry, and photography) is a major theme. Subsequently, an idea for a similar art activity will often spring unsolicited from the children who, after reading such books, are then eager to emulate the abilities of their newfound "friends."

Finally, to sustain the impetus of creating, children need a respectable vehicle through which to share their artistic products. An exhibition provides a perfect way for children to complete their learning process and to collect the praise and affirmation that causes them to value their own artistic efforts and abilities. By taking ownership of their exhibitions, from arranging their artworks to conceiving ways for the audience to respond, children begin to take themselves seriously as creative beings. Then they, too, like the fictional artists presented in this chapter, may feel they possess a true artist's vision.

QUESTIONS FOR JOURNAL WRITING AND DISCUSSION

1. In your opinion, what is the difference between children's responding to a piece of literature through art and using their art to stimulate writing? What memories do you recall of either situation from your elementary school years? Which were more positive for you? Why?

2. Think of a book you have read that had as a main character an artist or a musician, or select for reading one of the books mentioned in this chapter. How did the description of the artist's fascination for his or her art give you more openness and appreciation for trying the medium yourself? Why do you think this is so?

3. Discuss a product that you recently created (this could be a gourmet meal, a rock garden, a flower arrangement, a quilt, etc.). Explain what inspired you to execute the project and the steps you took to complete it. Describe your feelings about the finished product.

SUGGESTIONS FOR PROJECTS

1. Observe a group of kindergartners and a group of sixth graders involved in an art project. Make a list of what you see as the most obvious changes in the way children of different age groups express themselves.

2. Consult with a specialist in art in a school district. Determine how much of his or her planning is done in collaboration with the classroom teacher. Would the specialist prefer to work more closely with the classroom teacher? List some ways to facilitate teamwork between classroom teachers and specialists.

3. Read one of the following books mentioned in this chapter: *All I See, The Art Lesson, Julie's Daughter,* or *In Summer Light.* While reading your selection, examine your own responses to the main character's description of his or her artistic expression and feelings about it. Are you more inclined to want to attempt to express yourself using this medium? Design a lesson about the book that you feel would enhance children's enjoyment of the text by helping them internalize the love of art expressed by the main character.

REFERENCES

Cox, C., & Many, J. (1992). Toward an understanding of the aesthetic response to literature. *Language Arts, 69,* 28–33.

dePaola, T. (1989). *The art lesson.* New York: G. P. Putnam's Sons.

Dyson, A. H. (1986). The imaginary worlds of childhood: A multimedia presentation. *Language Arts, 63,* 799–808.

Morrow, L., Burks, S., & Rand, M. (1992). *Resources in early literacy development: An annotated bibliography.* Newark, DE: International Reading Association.

Oneal, Z. (1986). *In summer light.* New York: Bantam.

Rodowsky, C. (1985). *Julie's daughter.* New York: Farrar, Straus, & Giroux.

Rylant, C. (1988). *All I see.* New York: Orchard.

Stover, L. (1988). What do you mean, we have to read a book for art class? *Art Education, 41,* 9–17.

Szekely, G. (1988). The art exhibit as a teaching tool. *Art Education, 41,* 9–17.

Tyler, A. (1984). *Celestial navigation.* New York: Berkeley Books.

CHAPTER **6**

Living and Loving Poetry

Children are natural poets. This was recently reaffirmed for one of the authors by her 8-year-old daughter, who, watching the dry leaves in the middle of the road as the two were driving home, exclaimed, "Oh, look! The wind is hurrying the leaves across the road! The wind must be their mother!" Although most educators would be amused by this child's creative observations, not all would readily call it poetry. However, the present authors believe that if teachers could broaden their definition of the all-too-often esoteric term *poetry*, children might have a much better chance of understanding and creating poetry joyfully and successfully. By broadening our definition of poetry, rather than lowering expectations for the products, we would actually be expanding it to encompass all that children can hope to think or imagine—in any language. A poem could easily be:

- a riddle asked by the poet, who isn't there to tell the answer, or who doesn't know the answer, or doesn't care about the answer;
- mirrors in which poets see themselves;
- a stream of consciousness woven together from a million vague memories;
- a song in which poets furnish their own tune;
- the poet's most intimate thoughts in masquerade, which only those who care about the poet can recognize;
- a garden of words that might be planted in neat rows—but then again, they could grow wild and free; or
- a thought, experience, mood, observation, feeling, picture, idea, or question set in a personalized design of words.

Unfortunately, we often lose sight of the primacy of poetry in the elementary school in favor of other, more "down to earth" modes of discourse. Yet poetry, as the epitome of fine art, can be an invaluable resource for allowing children to express themselves intuitively, while providing excellent practice in the language arts of reading, writing, listening, and speaking.

CHOOSING POETRY TO SHARE WITH CHILDREN

Studies of how children are exposed to poetry at school suggest that teachers most often utilize only that poetry provided by the basal series that the children read in class, or that they use poems found in literature anthologies (Terry, 1974). Often these selections lack the extensive lesson planning guidance usually provided for stories by the instruction manual; therefore, the poems are generally read aloud to children by the teacher, skipped over entirely, or merely assigned for the children to memorize (Shapiro, 1990).

However, for children to begin to see poetry as an exciting and powerful vehicle for them to use to experiment with their own words, perceptions, and ideas, they must be continually surrounded by a wide range of poetic stimuli. Indeed, the sparse attention given to poetry in many classrooms leads children to believe that poetry is perhaps appropriate for special holidays, or a slight break from regular routine, but not much else.

M. F. Heller (1991) suggests that poetry be read aloud to children every single day so that they begin to tune in to its rhythm, repetition, and musiclike qualities, which are so close to a child's heart. She states that the poetic selections can be rhymed, unrhymed, nonsense verse, lyrical, or ballad, but that the nature of poetry must have some innate, immediate appeal to children. She further warns teachers against selecting poems that are beyond the developmental level of the children so that the meaning must laboriously be explained, or "explicated" for them. Such practices have led to a lasting resistance to reading and writing poetry for far too many children.

Carol Lynch-Brown and Carl Tomlinson (1993) have compiled a helpful set of criteria for teachers to consider when selecting appropriate poems to read to children:

- A variety of poems should be offered. Although children may seem to prefer certain contemporary poets, they will soon enjoy a wider variety of poems if they are exposed to diverse poets.
- The way ideas are expressed should cause the readers to look at a subject in a new and fresh way.
- Beautiful illustrations should not be deciding factors in the selection of a poetry anthology; collections should be evaluated on the basis of the quality of the individual poems.
- Selected poems should tie into the experiences children have had and not preach to them about what they "should" do.
- Poems should focus on the child's world and perspective, as well as universal ideas to which all ages can relate.
- Finally, selected poems should express fresh, worthy, and imaginative ideas.

The range of appropriate poems may be selected from classic poetry, such as Robert Louis Stevenson's "My Shadow," William Blake's "The Tyger," or poems written especially for children, such as selected works of Langston Hughes, Jack Prelutsky, John Ciardi, or Shel Silverstein. Additionally, any poem that is a special favorite of the teacher can be shared with the children with a personal preface about its significance for that teacher. Finally, children can be inspired and reassured as to their own ability to read, write, and understand poetry by listening to poems that have been composed by other children their own age. Copies of poems written by children in the teacher's past classes are an excellent resource; the magazines *Cricket* and *Highlights*, among others, carry a wide variety of original poetry written by children.

ORAL READING OF POETRY IN THE CLASSROOM

By its very nature, poetry is meant to be shared orally. When a classroom collection of poetry has been assembled, teachers can encourage children to read poems during silent reading time; children can then choose their favorite selections to read to each other in pairs. Paired oral reading can then progress to a weekly time when children look forward to sharing their new poetic discoveries with the rest of the class—individually or with their partners—to being greeted with responsive comments and appreciative applause.

Some teachers use a motivational device called "Poem in My Pocket" to further arouse interest in oral recitation of poetry. In this activity, children record favorite poems on a piece of paper, which is then placed in their pockets; during specified class times, or at lunch recess, another child, teacher, or classroom guest may ask any of the students, "What poem is in *your* pocket?" to which the child can then respond by reciting his or her poem for the other person.

Similarly, a poetry reading can be a rewarding extension of children's involvement with poetry recitation in the classroom (Shapiro, 1990). For this event, children can elect to read a favorite poem individually or with a partner, or they may arrange a choral reading of their selection.

Choral reading can include the entire class or groups of children responding to each other. Children can choose to read their poems as a solo, duet, quartet, or any other grouping that fits with the poetry they have selected. The four major kinds of choral speaking are (Bromley, 1991, p. 94):

> *Line-at-a-time*: A child or small group of children speaks a line or two, alternating with another child or group of children who speaks a line or two.
>
> *Antiphonal*: Two groups of children alternate in speaking a piece. Often males and females are grouped together, or voices are grouped according to pitch. Different effects can be achieved by using differing combinations of pitch.
>
> *Refrain*: One child speaks most of the lines with a group of children chiming in at the refrain.
>
> *Unison*: The entire group of children speaks all the lines together.

Children may be encouraged either to read or to memorize their poem for their poetry reading, whichever seems most comfortable to them. Poems can be practiced by reading them aloud in front of a mirror or in front of classmates, or by reading them privately into a tape recorder. When the children feel ready to "perform" their selections, they can decide how to "stage" their poetry reading using appropriate props, music, and/or actions to enhance the feeling of each poem. The teacher can consult with each individual or group to offer helpful suggestions or comments.

The culminating poetry reading can be a gala evening affair, with parents and community members invited via elaborate invitations, or it might be a more informal event requiring only another class or a couple of other staff members acting as an audience to lend their appreciation and applause.

An attractive class book of the chosen poetry selections will ensure lasting memories of a poetry reading. Likewise, videotaping the event can immortalize it while also allowing children to later critique their own performances in readiness for any future poetry readings.

IDEAS FOR CLASSROOM PRACTICE

When children have been continually exposed to poetry and when poetry abounds in the classroom to be read and shared, children become quite receptive to writing their own poetry. However, to help teachers launch a successful poetry-writing curriculum, a few essential guidelines are offered here (Koch, 1970):

1. Assign poetry writing to be completed *in school*. This way, it is not considered "drudgery," but rather a refreshing change from the classroom routine, and children can share their creative excitement with other "poets." If some children choose to write poetry outside of school, however, the teacher should be aware that those children who write poetry at home have successfully transferred the excitement and good feeling of writing poetry to other aspects of their lives. This is a cause for celebration.

2. Do not expect children to consistently rhyme their poetry. While repetition is natural for children, rhyming can be an onerous chore that can interfere with what they are really trying to say. Providing models of unrhymed poems as well as rhymed ones will suggest to children that either format is acceptable for them.

3. Allow children to walk around the classroom as they are creating. Children will often become inspired by other children's ideas and word choices; they may wish to borrow some of the others' thoughts. This is perfectly appropriate.

4. Do not correct or negatively criticize a child's work. If a line in a poem seems unclear, simply ask the child what is meant by it, or ask specific questions to help the child clarify his or her own meaning.

5. Free children to write in their own words—and not what they surmise *you* want to hear—by explaining to them that their poems can be "pretend" (as opposed to "silly," which they may interpret as a pejorative term) or "real." Such a preface will prevent children from offering such hackneyed lines as "green is as green as the grass" when they are attempting to be "serious" poets trying to conform to perceived adult standards.

CREATING POETS IN THE CLASSROOM

In general, the tenets of the Bay Area Writing Project have shown its proponents how to guide children through the five steps of prewriting, drafting, revising, editing, and finally, sharing a piece of writing. The entire spectrum of learners in today's classroom—from gifted to second-language learners to hard-to-motivate learners—can be encouraged to write poetry with a similar eight-step plan: (1) provide a literacy scaffold, or temporary writing framework, for a poetry pattern, (2) read examples of other children's work that have employed that scaffold, (3) write a group poem using the scaffold, (4) celebrate the product of the group's effort, (5) allow children to write their own compositions using the same scaffold, but only if they choose to use it (some very creative, or more "seasoned" poets may have their own agenda that they prefer to use), (6) revise, after soliciting feedback from a trusted peer editor, (7) edit, after a conference with the teacher, and (8) proudly share the finished poem with a number of appreciative audiences.

The literacy scaffold can be a kind of formula for writing a poem by imitating, to a greater or lesser degree, an existing poem, such as the following:

BEES

Bees are buzzy,
Bees are bright.
    Boisterous, belligerent,
    Bellicose, bad.
    Bashful, beautiful,
    Bewildering, bold.
Bees are bright,
Bees are buzzy.
       Nancy Lee Cecil

In the above example, children would be helped to see how the poet used a pattern of adjectives that all begin with the same letter, as well as how the ending couplet is a mirror image of the beginning couplet. Subsequently, children can be asked to select a favorite animal or object to write about as a group. One fourth-grade class decided to write about turtles (with the help of the dictionary):

TURTLES

Turtles seem timid,
Turtles seem tired.
    Tactful, tacky,
    Tardy, tough.
    Testy, tasteful,
    Terrified, trusting.
Turtles seem tired.
Turtles seem timid.

After much self-congratulating among these fourth-grade students, they were then primed to write their own individual poems.

A simple scaffold idea is to have children begin each line with "I dream . . ." or "I wish . . ." (Koch, 1970), or describe in each line the student's feelings about a particular color, as in this poem written by a fifth grader:

GRAY

Gray is the color of the mist;
Gray is riding on a Greyhound bus;
Gray is a lone seagull's cry;
Gray is the fog or a half-burned log;
Gray is old and tired.
Gray is not me!

José, grade 5

To motivate and to increase the gamelike quality of poetry, simple accessible rules can be added to the literacy scaffold. Using the "I dream . . ." scaffold, for example, teachers can ask children to make each line contain a color, a person, and a place, as manifested in the following poem:

I DREAM

I dream I dance with President Clinton on lush, green Oahu;
I dream Axl Rose and I start a rock group in Ohio;
I dream I am chasing my black cat, Inky, all the way to
Terabithia with Madonna;
And I dream I am woken up by Milo and Otis in
My own pink bedroom.

Svetlana, grade 5

The five senses can be used as another scaffold that will additionally tie in poetry writing with science. With this poem idea, children are asked to select a color and describe that color, using their five senses:

RED

Red smells like cinnamon in a bakery;
Red looks like blood in a gory movie (only
We know it's only ketchup!)
Red sounds like firecrackers on the Fourth of July;
Red tastes like taco sauce or jelly beans;
And red feels like anger when my older brother
Teases me.

Tasha, grade 3

Such literacy scaffolds and others that can be created by the teacher, using simple, easy to imitate ideas, can help children to feel immediately successful in their initial attempts at poetry writing. After peer editors have offered helpful suggestions and the teacher has praised and proofread the final product, children's proud creations can be incorporated into a class poetry book.

OTHER CLASSROOM USES FOR POETRY

Although teachers will want to scrupulously avoid "basalizing" poetry experiences by forcing children to continually explicate poems and derive certain esoteric meanings from them, some open-ended discussions of certain poems can enhance them for children. For example, after reading Robert Frost's "Stopping by Woods on a Snowy Evening," the teacher could ask, "Does the dark, snowy night in this poem remind you of any experiences in *your* life?" Similarly, after reading William Blake's "The Tyger," the teacher could casually query, "What animal would you most like to be? Why?" or "Which animal frightens you the most? Why?" Such personal and higher level discussions help children to come to terms with their own perceptions about a poem. Additionally, such discussions help children to internalize the poem and remember it longer and, as a result, make them more receptive to hearing and sharing poetry in the future.

Finally, because poetry is such a unique style of expression, it particularly lends itself to some very creative modes of presentation (Cecil, 1993):

1. Poems can be dramatized. Some poems, such as Frost's "The Road Not Taken," can be written on the chalkboard. Students can then read the poem aloud and divide into small groups to discuss their feelings about the poem. They can then be encouraged to act out their interpretations of the poem to be shared with the rest of the class.
2. Poems that have been selected by children can be recited chorally by breaking them up into individual lines or phrases. Participants write the poem on sturdy cardboard and then cut each line into a separate strip. To reassemble the poem each participant then selects a line. The children then stand in front of the class in the order in which their strip falls in the poem, and read their parts. The rest of the class may choose to join in.
3. Poems associated with certain holidays, moods, or seasons can be read to the class by individuals or groups of children. Sound effects evocative of the mood can be selected to highlight the poem. For example, sleigh bells could be jangled for a reading of " 'Twas the Night before Christmas," and "The Song of Hiawatha" might be enhanced by faint drum beats in the distance. Similarly, scary moans, groans, and maniacal laughter could send chills down the spines of listeners to a Halloween poem.

SUMMARY

Poetry is an exemplary vehicle through which children can come to appreciate the rhyme, rhythm, and repetition of the English language. A major commitment to poetry in an elementary classroom would include assembling a wide range of developmentally appropriate poems for children to listen to, read silently, and read to each other. Poems can be shared with classmates through drama, choral reading, and more formally through poetry readings for selected audiences.

This chapter provides a guide for making poetry an integral part of a joyous literacy program. It further includes suggestions for encouraging children to write their own poetry with the use of specific literacy scaffolds that allow each child access to his or her own ideas—regardless of English proficiency.

All young children have fresh and untested perceptions of the world. The authors of this text believe all children can be freed to write the most original and least self-conscious poetry with the help of a facilitating teacher. When children have learned to trust their own thoughts and have experienced their classmates' appreciation for their poems, they will begin to feel a heady success through this unique mode of discourse. When this happens, another avenue for literacy and self-expression has been tapped.

QUESTIONS FOR JOURNAL WRITING AND DISCUSSION

1. Obtain several poetry anthologies that are listed in the bibliography of children's literature in the appendix. Select one poem that especially appeals to you and read it to a small group of your classmates. Compare your feelings about the poem before and after you read it. What does the oral sharing of poetry do for appreciation? Why?

2. How do you feel about poetry? Discuss any positive or negative experiences you have had with poetry in the past. Describe steps you will take to make poetry a valued means of expression in your own classroom.

3. Share an experience you have had in school or college when a poem was "explicated" by the instructor. How did the explication make you feel about the poem? How did the experience change your feelings about poetry in general?

SUGGESTIONS FOR PROJECTS

1. Consider the following poem written by a fourth-grade boy whose assignment was to write about his feelings for a beloved pet:

    I have a beagle.
       He's not a sea gull.
          He's not even regal.

    Is this a creative response? Does the poem touch upon the feelings the boy has for his dog? Why or why not? Describe a prewriting exercise that might have enabled the boy to express his feelings about his pet.

2. Select one of the literacy scaffolds mentioned in this chapter. Brainstorm some ideas that you would like to use for a poem. Write your own poem using the topic you have chosen. Share your product with a friend or classmate to solicit feedback. Incorporate selected feedback and read the final product to a small share group. Describe the experience in your journal.

3. Examine a current basal reader series. How much poetry is included in it? Do the instructions for teachers provide helpful instructions for making the poem more enjoyable for children? Are suggestions included for teaching children to write poetry? Do you think this series would enable a teacher to instill in children a love for poetry?

REFERENCES

Bromley, K. D. (1991). *Webbing with literature: Creating story maps with children's books.* Boston: Allyn & Bacon.

Cecil, N. L. (1993). *Teaching to the heart: An affective approach to reading instruction.* Salem, WI: Sheffield.

Heller, M. F. (1991). *Reading-writing connections: From theory to practice.* White Plains, NY: Longman.

Koch, K. (1970). *Wishes, lies, and dreams.* New York: Chelsea House.

Lynch-Brown, C., & Tomlinson, C. M. (1993). *Essentials of children's literature.* Boston: Allyn & Bacon.

Shapiro, S. (1990). Beyond the anthology: Poetry readings in the classroom. In N. Cecil (Ed.), *Literacy in the 90's: Selected readings in the language arts* (pp. 122–127). Dubuque, IA: Kendall/Hunt.

Terry, A. (1974). *Children's poetry preferences: A national survey of the upper grades.* Champaign, IL: National Council of Teachers of English.

CHAPTER 7

Drama: Bringing Ideas to Life

As far back as this author can remember, children have been acting in school plays, dressing up as carrots (or bunnies or angels) on stages in stuffy auditoriums. Often, the children forget their lines or are unable to be heard beyond the second row. But everyone in the audience is delighted anyway. They think something special and wonderful is occurring, and they are right.

The inherent value of dramatic experiences for children, in general, has been cited by many proponents of this unique art form. Moreover, Brian Edmiston, Pat Encisco, and Martha King (1987) insist that drama should be considered the very core of language development and learning. Indeed, drama, more than most other art forms, has held a continuous place of honor in many language arts curricula, perhaps because creative teachers intuitively know that through drama (yes, even in the above scenario) children are working cooperatively toward a common goal, developing self-expression abilities, as well as fostering their creative imaginations and language facility. However, drama has some even more compelling qualities that can make it an ideal vehicle through which to reach the wide spectrum of culturally and linguistically diverse children who are often skirting the fringes of more traditional language arts activities. A committee sponsored by the National Endowment for the Arts recently concluded that:

- Drama offers a creative and psychological balance to more academic instruction.
- Drama is a magical experience that offers a playful way to look at reality.
- Drama is respectful of childhood in that it showcases a sense of pretending and wonder.
- Drama enhances ability in all other academic areas by making children better thinkers (Corathers, 1991).

Finally, Howard Gardner (1985) speculates that drama has some unique benefits as compared with other art forms. In other expressions of art, one is looking for sensitivity to specific types of patterns: sounds and rhythm in music, and visual configurations in the spatial arts. Drama, on the other hand, requires a different kind of sensitivity, or intelligence. Highlighted in drama is an incisive ability to size up very quickly what is going on in an environment. Gardner goes on to suggest that while other disciplines, such as music or math, require children to think and respond in isolation, with very little knowledge of the outside world, theater underscores an entirely different kind of intelligence that is inherently interpersonal in nature. Drama affords children the opportunity to experience the most rewarding social aspects of language and nonverbal communication because they interact with the audience on one level and with their fellow cast members on another, more immediate level.

DRAMA FOR A DIVERSE CLASSROOM

Cecily O'Neill (1989) argues that drama in which teacher and students cocreate fictional roles and content has a great deal of potential for promoting rich and meaningful dialogue that will allow all children to reflect upon and explore routine issues or events. For example, to help primary children become more sensitive to the anxieties held by children who are new to a school, or new to a culture, O'Neill suggests that children take on the role of teachers at the school while the teacher, student teacher, and aides or parent helpers become the children. The children take such a radical reversal of usual roles very seriously. Through the interpretation of facial expressions and gestures on the part of the "children" and many kind words and helpful deeds by the "teachers," the "children" become more comfortable in their strange surroundings. The ensuing debriefing discussion makes it clear to observers that children have been challenged to understand a common situation in a new and profound way.

The magic of drama when used in the preceding way is that it asks participants and audience alike to hold two discrete planes in their mind at the same time: what is visually unfolding, or what is "fiction," and what is being symbolically portrayed, or what is "real." To illustrate this point, Gavin Bolton (1984) uses an example of a person playing the role of someone being interviewed. The observers watch with rapt attention the person playing the interviewee, knowing full well that the role-player is only pretending, yet responding as if he or she is not. Holding both of these planes in mind at the same time can bring about added insights in children's perceptions and ideas of the world around them. Moreover, the exaggerated emphasis on the context in which the actor is shown, in this case an interview situation, aids the limited English-speaking children in grasping the ideas more readily than they otherwise could, thus allowing them easier access to the content of what is being explored.

BUILDING COMMUNITY THROUGH IMPROVISATION

All drama, in the highest sense, can be a form of actual verbal and nonverbal language laboratory for the elementary classroom in that it can involve children in conceptualizing ideas and developing alternative ways of communicating whether the children are English as a Second Language (ESL) learners doing so for the first time or native speakers seeking a new voice (Shaw, 1976). To best epitomize the language laboratory in the elementary classroom, teachers can introduce improvisational exercises that will build a sense of cooperation and trust; such exercises also allow children to develop the skills necessary to translate written and oral ideas into actions (Spolin, 1962). Moreover, improvisational games are considered ideal precursors to more formalized drama.

The first improvisational exercise that might be introduced is simple: children stand in a circle and pass around an imaginary basketball. The second time around, the ball turns into an object. The children pass the object from person to person without telling each other what the object is, but rather suggesting its identity by the way they handle it. The third time around, the object transforms itself into energy from inside the children's own bodies. Each child accepts the energy from a neighbor, moves it to a part of his or her own body, and then passes it on. The fourth time around, the energy is turned into sound. The same procedure ensues: each child accepts the sound from a neighbor and then passes it along as a different sound. The fifth and final time around, the sound is changed into a word. Each child repeats the word received from a neighbor, changes it into any word that comes into his or her head, and then passes the word on (Spolin, 1962).

A second exercise invites children to view a picture or painting of a group of people. An example might be the family group of seven people and a dog in Thomas Hovendon's "Breaking Home Ties" (Figure 7.1). A group of seven children talk about the painting and discuss what is happening in the painting:

> Why does everyone look so sad?
>
> Where is the boy going?
>
> What is the woman saying to the boy?
>
> How are the two people in the doorway involved in the event?

Each child in the group then selects one of the characters in the painting and "becomes" that character, donning the character's mood, thoughts, and demeanor. The children arrange themselves in a "frieze," as similar to the painting as possible, and then develop a conversation that they imagine might take place among the characters.

One group of seven fourth-grade students created the following dialogue to accompany their frieze:

MOTHER: Robert, why must you go? There is a blizzard and you're going to catch cold.

FIGURE 7.1

SOURCE: Thomas Hovendon's "Breaking Home Ties" from the Philadelphia Museum of Art: Given by Ellen Harrison McMichael in memory of C. Emory McMichael.

SON: Mom, you know I need to ask for some money at the bank. We are very poor.

YOUNG WOMAN [*seated, petting dog*]: Well, I could lend you some money. I've been saving money I usually spend on dog food because Fluffy has been catching lots of rabbits to eat.

FLUFFY: Ruff!

MAN [*with back to others*]: Come on, Robert. We'd better hurry before it gets dark.

OLD WOMAN [*seated*]: Yes, Robert, hurry before it gets any darker. The roads will be quite slippery. You know how much I worry!

YOUNG WOMAN [*standing*]: Robert, why don't you let me go with you?

MAN [*at door, looking at Robert*]: No, Laura. Thanks, but you'd better stay here and take care of your mother. When we get back, if we've managed to get the money, we'll celebrate with some hot chocolate. Now let's be off, Robert!

A third improvisational exercise involves creating an environment. Placing all students in an unfamiliar situation helps to bring about a feeling of empathy and harmony within the class. For such an exercise, the class is divided in half. Each half is instructed to create a known environment for the other half to identify and then cohabit. The dramatic portrayal of the environment must take into account not only the physical place, but also the concomitant people, animals, and vegetation that might live or work there. For example, if one group decides to create a jungle, the group members must consider and act out all aspects of jungle life. One student may don the role of a monkey, while two others are vines and three more are the Amazon River. When each group has finished creating its environment, one group goes first and "performs" it in a dynamic and living way. The group watching is told to watch closely and try to figure out what the environment might be. Once the children think they have guessed, they are encouraged to actively participate with the actors, becoming new jungle characters, such as a hut, a missionary, a boa constrictor, or whatever they feel will fit into the framework of that environment. As each child joins in, the small group soon becomes the whole class again. The second group then performs its environment using the same process. A discussion follows, describing what worked and did not work in portraying the environment and evaluating the experience. A heightened sense of community, as well as a better appreciation of nuances of nonverbal communication, is fostered (Spolin, 1962).

A fourth improvisational exercise is a classic theater technique called "The Mirror." Children are put into pairs and face one another. They are told to think of the pair as one person looking into a full-length mirror: the second child is the mirror image of the first. After the two children take a few minutes to examine each other, staring into each other's eyes, the second child must mirror what the first child does as the action occurs. The first child should not make sudden or jerky movements to throw the mirror off, but should offer slow, graceful movements that will give the second child a chance to follow. Then, without speaking, the mirror and the first child change roles, and the first child becomes the mirror. A new level of nonverbal communication is realized as one child attempts to sense what the other is feeling and about to do, while the other child tries to facilitate the silent communication.

BRINGING LITERATURE TO LIFE

The improvisational exercises just described can be an excellent catalyst for other forms of drama in the classroom, because such activities not only enhance interest in other forms of symbolic representations, but also foster positive interaction with peers. After some experience with improvisation, children are usually eager to move from almost exclusively nonverbal enactments to drama using words. They are ready to improvise skits.

Skits can be devised when a class reads a story together or when one is read to them by the teacher. Afterward the teacher asks the children to recount the scenes they liked best. Ordinarily, the children will tend to choose those that the teacher has already deemed appropriate for them to dramatize (this isn't as unlikely as it seems; children are most drawn to scenes with the most intensity—the funniest, saddest, or most exciting—which lend themselves to dramatic reenactment).

After the story has been read and discussed, the first step toward bringing it to life involves retelling the story. For example, a class has chosen to dramatize the graveyard scene from *The Adventures of Tom Sawyer*. The teacher asks, "Who would like to tell what happened to Tom and Huck in the graveyard?" A child who volunteers to relate the story might begin, "Well, Tom and Huck are hiding behind this tree, and then they see a light coming. They don't know what it is, so they stay very still." When the child finishes retelling the events in the scene, other class members can be encouraged to add important details. When children have finished recounting the story in their own words, the teacher can ask probing questions designed to have the children reflect more deeply about the feelings and motivations of the characters.

Questions such as the following, for example, would help children to think about the motivations of the main characters: "How do you think Tom and Huck were feeling when they were hiding behind the tree in the graveyard?" "Did Huck feel the same way Tom did? How do you know?" "Did he show it in the same way?" Such questions will make possible a more sensitive portrayal of the character.

When the children have finished retelling all the events in the scene and have talked about how the characters were feeling, they are ready to discuss characterization. An effective technique to begin this phase is pantomime. The children take turns silently acting out, with broad actions and facial gestures, any character in the scene they choose. The rest of the class must guess which character is being impersonated. Children should be encouraged to think about the character's state of mind, whether he or she is young or old, bold or shy, mean or kind, and how such attributes might affect the character's walk, gestures, and expressions. If children are having trouble understanding a character's particular trait or mood, an impromptu scene can help. For example, if children are having difficulty portraying Tom frightened in the graveyard, the teacher might suggest: "Imagine you and your little sister are home alone one night and suddenly you hear a rattle on the living room window. Show how you would move. How would your voice sound? What might you say to your little sister?"

After internalizing the feelings of the characters, the children will be ready to act out the scene. Although some may be shy and hesitant at first, it does not take long for the most outgoing few to volunteer to begin improvising. The teacher can facilitate most effectively by sitting on the sidelines and allowing the children to resolve how each segment might be played, with an occasional prompt such as, "Now here come Doc and Injun Joe and Muff," to make a bridge to the next section. It is also helpful for the teacher to ask the rest of the class not to interrupt the scene with suggestions; the actors should feel free to play it "their way" (Durland, 1975).

When the scene seems to be winding down toward the end, the teacher can affirm the performance by standing up, applauding, and then giving very specific positive feedback to each of the actors (e.g., "I like the way you showed that you were old, Doc, by bending over just a bit and talking in a quavery voice.") By now other children will be eager to try the same scene, having had the opportunity to observe and reflect on how they might alter the performance of a certain character. The scene can then be repeated until all who wish to do so have had an opportunity to share their interpretation of a character in the scene.

At this juncture the play has essentially cast itself, for even the most reticent children (who often display surprising dramatic talent) have had a chance to act out a part or two, and children can intelligently and democratically vote for the children who they feel have best captured the different flavors of the characters. When children have seen all their classmates perform, they will then generally avoid simply voting for their friends or the most popular children. Moreover, with the children themselves doing the casting, there are no nerve-wracking tryouts with resultant hurt feelings, which can occur when teachers cast the play according to who they feel would be best in the play.

When the casting has been completed, the teacher—or in upper grades, a student—can write down the script on a ditto master, using the children's own dialogue and perhaps adding a few stage directions in parentheses. Children are usually delighted to recognize their own words; the script becomes a reading activity superior to any language-experience lesson. Moreover, children have the incentive to read the script over and over until it has been memorized, thus ensuring much needed practice on basic sight vocabulary and phrasing.

Such an adapted script has many advantages over commercial scripts: The language approximates children's own, and the lines are rarely too lengthy or too difficult. Additionally, the scene will usually be the appropriate length, rhythm, and complexity for the group of children that has created it.

CREATING ORIGINAL DRAMA

Perhaps the most exciting and language-enriching dramatic activities in elementary classrooms are the productions that are written and developed by the children themselves. When children move from acting out the ideas of others to bringing their own thoughts to life, they experience the heady pride associated with ownership of a project from start to finish.

As creating scripts is one of the most ambitious tasks that can be undertaken in drama, certain steps should be followed to ensure a satisfying transition from adapting the works of others to trying their hands at play writing. For this reason, the following suggestions may be helpful to consider: (1) Start small, encourage children to begin with rudimentary one-act skits; (2) Allow children to work in small groups. Dividing a class of 28 children into four groups of 7 will make more equitable creative interchange possible for all group members, rather than only the most vociferous; and (3) Provide several motivational prompts, or plot ideas for each group to consider. Giving specific "germs" to children offers them a structure to build upon and inspires them (Cecil, 1987). Following the drafting of the skit, the revising and editing stages can be undertaken using feedback from peer editors from other small groups.

Following are examples of motivational play-writing prompts that have been field-tested and found to stimulate intermediate children to write original skits:

1. Three friends are playing catch in one friend's backyard. Suddenly, the children look up in the sky and see a spaceship that soon lands about five feet away from them. Several aliens emerge from the spaceship and salute the surprised children. One of the aliens invites the children to come on board with the aliens.
   a. Are the aliens friendly or unfriendly?
   b. What do they want from the children?
   c. Where do the aliens want to take the children?
   d. How will the children return to earth?
2. Seven farm animals—a turkey, a horse, a cow, a chicken, a goat, a sheep, and a pig—decide that their barnyard lives are too dull. The animals make a pact that they will take turns going outside the barnyard in pursuit of adventure. When they return, they then take turns sharing their adventures. Each one then decides whether to leave the barnyard.
   a. What are the adventures of each animal?
   b. Which, if any, animals decide to stay in the barnyard? Why?
   c. What have the animals learned from their adventures?
3. Three children are discussing what they would wish for if they could have anything they wanted. A magic genie appears and tells them that, among the three of them, they will be granted three wishes.
   a. What do the children decide to wish for?
   b. Do the children's wishes come true?
   c. What happens to each of the children when the wishes do or do not come true?

After the teacher has helped each group brainstorm some ideas about the prompt that they have chosen or another that they have made up themselves, a recorder in each group can write down the ideas on paper. The teacher can assist by explaining the conventions peculiar to play writing—for example, that actions concomitant with the dialogue are written parenthetically. Casting the actors for the original skits is often easier than it is for the adapted skits because children generally create the same number of characters as there are in the group and usually "become" the character they were most instrumental in creating.

IDEAS FOR CLASSROOM PRACTICE

A few suggestions may help teachers to avoid some of the most common pitfalls of putting on plays, whether they are adapted or original scripts:

1. Do not allow adults to "overproduce" the skit. All too many elementary school productions are replete with community orchestra, backgrounds done professionally by the school's art instructors, elaborate costumes designed by enthusiastic parents, and dazzling makeup that is uncomfortable or runs into the children's eyes under the hot lights. In order for children to retain maximum ownership over what should be *their* production, it is far better to keep the skit as simple as possible, with child-made backgrounds and a few basic props such as hats, aprons, or canes to merely suggest the characters. Makeup is not necessary. In this way the strength of the dramatic production will depend on the children's own actions and oral interpretation of the characters, rather than on the more illusory trappings of the would-be Hollywood set.

2. Encourage children to add music and dance to the production in ways that are comfortable and familiar to them. Offer the suggestion that they may choose familiar songs or other musical compositions to add to the full expression of their characters. Similarly, invite children to demonstrate the various moods or states of mind of their characters through broad body movements to accompany the musical selections. As an example, one class of fourth graders improvised a skit from the previously described prompt about aliens landing in their backyard. They decided they would like to use *2001: A Space Odyssey*, a theme that had been played in class on numerous occasions. The children felt that the music fit the surrealistic event of an encounter with beings from outer space. In their skit, the creators had the four aliens emerge from their spacecraft in dreamy, ethereal movements choreographed to the pulse of the music.

3. Avoid using adult prompters. Traditionally, parents or the children's teacher remain in the stage wings during the final dramatic production, as well as during earlier rehearsals, to ensure that if children forget their lines they will not be stranded. However, if no such "safety net" is offered, children willingly begin to learn from each other's lines and, in a truly cooperative environment, may be depended upon to remind each other of temporarily forgotten phrases. Moreover, if children are always encouraged to be mindful of the gist of what they are saying in logical sequence rather than the mere parroting of lines in isolation, they can be taught to ad lib their lines and not to worry if the exact script does

not come to mind. In either of these alternatives, the onus of language development, which is at the core of the activity, is put squarely on the shoulders of the children rather than on the prompter's.

SUMMARY

Drama can be a highly effective mode of self-expression through which children can develop their communication abilities while fostering their creative imaginations. Furthermore, children for whom English is a second language can more clearly begin to grasp concepts and have access to a variety of ideas through a unique and compelling art form.

Improvisational exercises can be considered the precursors to actual dramatic productions because they build a heightened sense of community spirit while having children focus on the nonverbal aspects of communication. By allowing the teacher and children to switch roles on occasion, children become better able to see another's point of view. Bringing literature to life by using adapted scripts can help children to internalize the motivation of characters while ensuring a long-lasting memory and appreciation of the story. Finally, original skits can be the best means through which children can apply all facets of language—reading, writing, listening, and speaking—in a creative thinking endeavor that is highly enjoyable.

Overall, expanding language capabilities through drama is the ultimate avenue for developing thinking and feeling individuals. The creative release manifested through drama, regardless of whether there is true "talent" or not, brings about a free flow of energy that in turn will often ignite other creative abilities. Through such activities, the lives of both the children and the teacher have been profoundly enriched.

QUESTIONS FOR JOURNAL WRITING AND DISCUSSION

1. Have you ever been in a dramatic production? Describe your experiences. Compare the production with the suggestions for production offered in this chapter.
2. Tell in your own words why drama and pantomime are ideal devices to integrate literacy and the arts in classrooms containing second-language speakers. Compare and contrast a classroom that uses much drama with a more traditional classroom.
3. Respond to this statement in the text: "Drama enhances ability in all other academic areas by making children better thinkers" (Corathers, 1991, p. 2). How might drama help children become better thinkers in such curricular areas as social studies? Science? Math?

SUGGESTIONS FOR PROJECTS

1. Select one of the improvisational exercises mentioned in this chapter. Plan to teach this exercise to a group of children or a group of your classmates. Follow the improvisation with a discussion about the value of nonverbal communication.

2. With a group of classmates, reenact the skit about becoming more sensitive to the anxiety of children new to a school or culture. In a second reenactment, reverse the roles of teachers and children. Discuss non-English speaking children's dependence on facial expressions and gestures.

3. Select a fine art painting from an art appreciation book listed in the bibliography of children's literature in the appendix. With classmates, prepare a frieze of this work with concomitant dialogue. Share the frieze with other members of the class.

4. Select a folk or fairy tale that you feel would be suitable for dramatic exploration at the 3–6 grade level and devise a plan for acting it out using the suggestions outlined in this chapter.

REFERENCES

Bolton, G. (1984). *Drama as education: An argument for placing drama at the center of the curriculum.* Harlow, Essex: Longman.

Cecil, N. L. (1993). Reading through creative drama. In *Teaching to the heart: An affective approach to reading instruction* (pp. 77–86). Salem, WI: Sheffield.

Corathers, D. (Nov. 1991). Theater education: Seeking balance between stage and classroom. *ASCD Curriculum Update.*

Durland, F. C. (1975). *Creative dramatics for children: A practical manual for teachers and leaders.* Kent, OH: Kent State University Press.

Edmiston, B., Enciso, P., & King, M. L. (1987). Empowering readers and writers through drama: Narrative theater. *Language Arts, 64,* 219–229.

Gardner, H. (1985). Towards a theory of dramatic intelligence. In J. Kase-Polisini (Ed.), *Creative drama in a developmental context* (pp. 295–312). New York: University Press of America.

O'Neill, C. (1989). Dialogue and drama: The transformation of events, ideas, and teachers. *Language Arts, 66,* 147–159.

Shaw, A. M. (1976). Improvisational drama and language growth. In P. Finn & W. T. Petty (Eds.), *Creative dramatics in the language arts classroom.* Report of the Second Annual Conference on Language Arts Education, State University of New York, Buffalo.

Spolin, V. (1962). *Improvisation for the theater.* Evanston, IL: Northwestern University Press.

CHAPTER **8**

The Singing of Songs

One of the authors confesses that from the age of 5 to 6½ she was a joyful singer of songs. She reminisces:

"At age 5 I attended kindergarten, where the teacher sang and taught us songs. I will always remember my introduction to songs such as:

2. And everywhere that Mary went... the lamb was sure to go.
3. It followed her to school one day... which was against the rule.
   Spoken: "No lambs at school!"

I so enjoyed singing. It was a new and wonderful experience for me. Throughout kindergarten and first grade, I continued my joyful enthusiastic singing. One day I was confidently holding the last note of a song when the visiting music specialist walked by and remarked to the first-grade teacher, 'She has a lovely voice.' The first-grade teacher grimaced and replied, 'But she can't carry a tune.' I was completely devastated. I stopped singing.

"For so many years, my joy of singing was locked up inside of me, until I became a teacher of parents in a class attended by both the parents and their preschool children. It was the practice in the community college where I taught to have a daily songtime using a big, illustrated songbook of the district's collection of simple songs. I found that with extensive practice I could carry the tunes of the simple songs. I could also hide behind the big songbook and feel less self-conscious, since attention was diverted to the picture rather than focused on me. I again became a joyful singer of songs. The parents and their preschool children joined in. We became a community of singers!"

BUILDING A COMMUNITY OF SINGERS

The singing of songs should be an integral part of the lives of all children. Singing should be as natural as talking (Davidson, McKernon, & Gardner, 1981). Preschools operate on this principle, and daily group song times include spirited renditions of favorite tunes. But when children reach elementary school, music is often regarded as a frill and is taught once a week by a music specialist. Is this relegation of music to secondary status the result of a narrow curriculum focused on academic skills? Is it bolstered by discomfort on the part of nonsinging teachers who feel that singing is a special talent that they do not possess and are therefore not qualified to teach? Or is this attitude the result of an educational system that considers singing the realm of the gifted and talented and relegates the rest of us to the passive role of audience (Gardner, 1989)? In answer to the above questions, this chapter maintains that children and adults need *not* be skillful performers to become joyful singers of songs.

Joyful singers of songs learn much more than "just singing." The whole child is involved. Children grow socially by learning to collaborate in the production of a song. They grow emotionally through the opportunity to express and appreciate feelings in a powerful mode. They develop coordination and control by responding physically to music through such simple experiences as clapping to rhythms and moving to the beat. For those more interested in intellectual learning, children benefit tremendously from experience with the words and music of songs. With appropriate guidance and extensions by the teacher, children can learn new vocabulary and concepts that lead to musical knowledge, language development, and literacy. For children who have special language needs such as language delays, and for students with limited English or those who are learning English as a second language, songs with their rhyme, rhythm, and repetition are particularly potent paths to language competence and literacy (Jalongo & Bromley, 1984).

SINGING AND ORAL LANGUAGE DEVELOPMENT AT THE PRESCHOOL AND KINDERGARTEN LEVELS

Simple songs, nursery rhymes set to music, folk music, and songs with motions and sound effects comprise the repertoire of music in the preschool and kindergarten. Adding simple appropriate illustrations to the songs and creating a big picture songbook can greatly enhance young children's language learning during song time (Figure 8.1). Children are wonderful imitators, and though the words of a song can be parroted, the result is rote learning (Graham, 1985). To promote concept learning, teachers need to involve children actively. Clear pictures identified with each song in a large, illustrated songbook to be used with the whole class provide the opportunity for discussions relating the words of the song to the children's own vocabularies and experiences. These discussions result in the construction of conceptual knowledge. The use of pictures also facilitates the reinforcement of multisensory modes of learning—visual as well as auditory, and at times even kinesthetic (for example, when circular hand motions are used for "the wheels on the bus" that go round and round).

During daily group song time with a big picture songbook, children can participate and practice at their own level with no pressure to demonstrate their skill (or lack thereof) as is required for solo singing. In the beginning children will listen to the songs, look at the pictures, and observe any accompanying movements. Participation may start with the motions or sound effects and, after some time has elapsed, end with an enthusiastic singing of the songs. Labels can be placed next to the pictures to promote print awareness. If the songbook is laminated and children

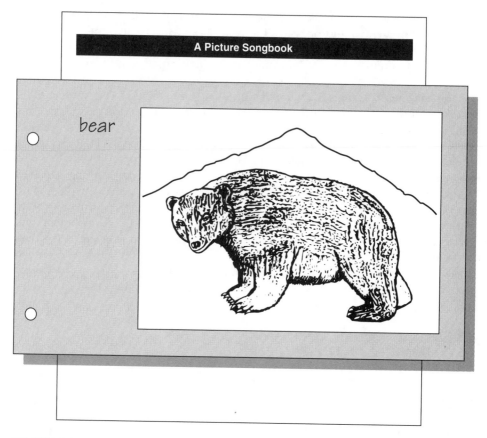

A Picture Songbook

bear

FIGURE 8.1

SOURCE: Phyllis Lauritzen "The Bear Went Over The Mountain" from the *Preschool Song Kit*. Copyright 1982. Reprinted by permission.

are allowed to look at it during free choice time, this will become a popular child-initiated activity.

Following the model of a teacher who sings "The Swinging Song" (Lauritzen, 1982) as the children are rhythmically swinging, children will spontaneously burst into song throughout the school day, create their own versions of familiar tunes, and even put original chants to music. J. J. Holahan (1985) suggests that "because the child can create music, it seems reasonable to suggest that music syntax, like language syntax, is a generative capacity" (p. 112). Thus, the singing of songs can become part of each child's life, not just a group time activity.

Guidelines for Teachers Who Wish to Become Song Leaders

1. Enthusiasm and a willingness to experiment are the essential requirements of a successful song leader. The goal is not a professional quality performance but rather an authentic enjoyment of singing.

2. Selecting songs to match the developmental level of the singers is critical. For young beginning singers, short songs that have distinct rhythms, understandable lyrics, repetitive patterns, and sound effects or hand motions, and that also require a limited vocal range of five notes from D to A, are developmentally appropriate (Alper, 1987; McDonald, 1979; Miller, 1987). Examples might include traditional lullabies, finger plays, nursery rhymes, call-and-response songs, and songs about the everyday experiences of children (see Cole & Calmenson, 1991; Durrell, 1989; Glazer, 1990; Hart, 1992; Jenkins, 1966; Lauritzen, 1982; National Gallery of Art, 1991). For more experienced singers, appropriate contemporary rap music and popular songs as well as folk songs from countries all over the world can be included in the class's repertoire (Delacre, 1989; Haywood, 1966). Folk songs are part of our musical heritage, have been tested by generations, and are still constantly evolving. They provide a flexibility and an authenticity that communicate well with children (Cockburn, 1991). If children from different racial and ethnic groups are students in the class, teachers can ask the families to contribute songs in their native languages and dialects for everyone to learn and appreciate.

3. Practice the songs over and over by singing along with a record, a professional tape, or a personal tape made by a friend whose singing is admired. This promotes the overlearning necessary for a smooth performance. Group singing led by the teacher independent of prerecorded music allows for personal adjustment to the present group of participants.

4. A big picture songbook prepared with uncluttered, tasteful illustrations for each song not only stimulates discussions and oral language development, but also facilitates the formation of concepts. The songbook can be either teacher-made or chosen from those commercially available (Jalongo & Collins, 1985; Lamme, 1979, 1990; Lauritzen, 1982). Older children enjoy creating their own illustrations. See also the bibliography of children's literature in the appendix for complete books that illustrate one folk song and are increasingly becoming available.

5. Sit on a low chair close to the children, who are seated on a rug in a semicircle, and hold the picture songbook so that all can see. This provides a physical setting that facilitates the group song time.

6. Introduce a new song by saying something like "We are going to learn a song about a bear. Have any of you seen a bear?" This relates the subject of the song to the children's own experiences. The children can even growl like a bear to introduce the song. Seeger (1980) suggests that when singing a new song, do not sing it once but keep it going, singing it on and on in one uninterrupted song experience. This allows the song leader to feel more at ease with the song and gives the children time to become familiar with it.

7. Consult the children in the selection of songs and watch the children for clues as to their continued interest so that the song time is matched

to the children's tastes, moods, and attention spans. However, do not expect all children to sing as part of the group. Receptive learning takes place first, and children at their own individual rates will eventually participate, perhaps in the beginning with the sound effects or motions and finally with singing.

8. Introduce concepts appropriate to the children's stages of development to facilitate learning about music (Andress, 1985). Younger children are limited to basic concepts of loud and soft, fast and slow. By age 5, children can identify long and short tones, and high and low pitch. They have also progressed from choosing their own pitch to attempting to match given pitch contours (Davidson et al., 1981; Jalongo & Collins, 1985; McDonald, 1979). In other words, they can begin to carry a tune.

SINGING AND LITERACY IN THE PRIMARY GRADES

In the early primary grades, singing songs not only promotes language and an awareness of the joys of music, but also facilitates literacy development through a gradual transition from an illustrated songbook to song charts (Figure 8.2). Song charts, similar to language-experience stories, are developed with the children singing the words and the teacher writing them down. The children, depending upon their individual levels, illustrate the song or copy the chart to make individual or class songbooks (Barclay & Walwer, 1992).

Original songs composed by the children can also be encouraged. Improvisation often begins with the words and the melody of a familiar song such as "The Bear Went Over the Mountain" used as a template for the creation of new verses. Stimulated by a teacher who asks, "Who else could go over the mountain?" or "What else could the bear see on the other side?" the children modify the songs and create new verses (McCracken & McCracken, 1986). The original songs can then be included in the singing repertoire of the class and, with illustrations, can become part of the class songbook, a prized addition to the class library to be circulated in class or checked out and taken home to share with parents.

Songs not only use a symbol system to record lyrics; songs also have their *own* symbol system to record the music. Howard Gardner (1983), in his theory of multiple intelligences, speaks of music as one of the seven intelligences with its own symbol system. Musical notation positions notes on a linear staff; movement up and down the staff denotes tones of the scale. Playing a melody on a xylophone held vertically visually reinforces the melodic pattern of the song. Leading a song with hand motions that imitate the ups and downs of the melody provides further reinforcement. Recording the musical notation afterward on a chart introduces children to the symbol system of music (Figure 8.3). Reading music can be a gradually acquired skill for children in grades 2 and 3. In addition to reading the lyrics and the music, mathematics is involved in deciphering the time and the rhythm; thus, three intelligences—musical, linguistic, and mathematical—are integrated in reading a vocal score.

A SONG CHART: THE WORDS

The Bear Went Over The Mountain

The bear went over the mountain.

The bear went over the mountain.

The bear went over the mountain

To see what he could see.

(Spoken) "And what did he see?"

The other side of the mountain.

The other side of the mountain.

The other side of the mountain

Was all that he did see.

FIGURE 8.2

IDEAS FOR CLASSROOM PRACTICE

The following ideas will help a classroom teacher connect singing with linguistic and musical literacy learning:

1. Select a song that is a familiar favorite of the children and that contains simple words with rhyme, rhythm, and repetition to provide the best vehicle for promoting beginning literacy.
2. Link the words of the song to print by writing the lyrics on a song chart. Lead the group in singing the song one phrase at a time, and model strategies for sounding out words by thinking out loud as the lyrics are written down.

A SONG CHART: WORDS AND MUSIC

The Bear Went Over The Mountain

1. The   bear went o-ver the moun-tain. The bear went o-ver the moun-tain. The
2. The   o- ther side of the moun-tain. The o - ther side of the moun-tain. The

1. bear went o-ver the moun-tain to see what he could   see.
2. o- ther side of the moun-tain was all that he did   see.

Spoken between verse 1 and verse 2: "And what did he see?"

FIGURE 8.3

SOURCE: From Phyllis Lauritzen. (1982). *Preschool Song Kit*. Rio Vista, CA: Ways and Means Curriculum.

3. Invite the children to sing along once the chart is completed, and use a pointer to match each syllable of the words with a musical note to accentuate the rhythm of the song. (The old bouncing ball of community singing.)
4. Use the chart to highlight repetitious words and phrases and provide an opportunity to build sight vocabulary.
5. Encourage the creation of new lyrics by matching words that have the appropriate number of syllables to the rhythmic structures of the song. Scaffolds can be developed to help students get started by brainstorming possible variations on the words of the song. For example, McCracken & McCracken (1986) elicit names of other animals to substitute for the fox

in a box in the song "A-Hunting We will Go." The suggestions are then used as column headings with rhyming words listed below. The children form sensible rhymes from this rhyme bank to create new verses. A pocket chart with the words of the original song can be used to test the new verses' fit.

6. For children in grades 2 and 3, develop a *musical* song chart that includes both the lyrics and the musical notation to connect previous learnings to the symbol system of music (Weil, 1989). Introduce the concept of ascending and descending melody by directing singing with up-and-down hand motions. This leads to writing the melody's contours with notes of the scale on a musical staff. Children learn that these notes of the scale have names, specified positions on the staff, and a corresponding pitch. They learn that a note of melody may be held for various lengths of time and that the rhythm of music is determined by the number of beats in a measure. Just as authors write words for readers, composers write notes on a staff for singers to sing or musicians to play on musical instruments.

SINGING IN THE INTERMEDIATE GRADES

In grades 3–6, some students are ready to build on strong foundations of positive dispositions toward music and may wish to engage in concentrated, in-depth skill development in either vocal or instrumental music (Gardner, 1989). For these students, focused practice through participation in an orchestra, band, glee club, chorus, or one-time projects such as the staging of a musical production should be available options. For all students, however, frequent singing opportunities should continue to be an integral part of the class curriculum. Further musical skill development for the whole class, such as the improvement of tonal quality, the use of different singing registers, breathing techniques, and aural imagery, can be developed in the regular music program through the use of musical selections that demand the appropriate level of competence. Thus, specific skill development can be integrated into the songs being sung (Hammer, 1978). This contextual teaching avoids the isolated skill development that Gardner (1981) fears can be the beginning of the end of musical development.

The approach to music suggested by this text makes the joy of singing accessible to all, not just a select group of talented performers. Additionally, because academic learnings can be embedded in singing-related activities, there can be no excuse for not integrating singing into the classroom and making "I can sing" a part of every child's self-concept.

SUMMARY

Singing should be a natural part of children's lives. In preschool and early childhood programs, a teacher who enthusiastically schedules daily songfests using a large picture songbook promotes not only singing but also conceptual and linguistic development. For children who are learning English as a second language, the rhyme, rhythm, and repetition of the songs are particularly potent paths for learning.

In kindergarten and the early primary grades, picture songbooks are replaced with song charts similar to language-experience stories. The song charts can be developed so that the children sing the song and the teacher writes the words. Concepts of print are expanded to include the idea that the words of songs can be written down; thus, literacy as well as linguistic and musical ability is enhanced.

When children are in the second and third grades, song charts can be further extended to include both the lyrics and the musical notation that introduces the symbol system of music. In the upper elementary grades some students, building on these basic skills, may wish to engage in concentrated lessons in either vocal or instrumental music; however, for all students, singing opportunities should continue to be a joyous, integral part of the curriculum.

QUESTIONS FOR JOURNAL WRITING AND DISCUSSION

1. What are your personal feelings about your singing ability? What experiences in your life caused you to acquire this feeling?
2. As a child did you have any kind of music lessons? If you did, did you enjoy this experience? Why or why not? If you did not, do you wish you had? Why or why not?
3. What were your favorite songs during your years in elementary school? Why did these songs appeal to you? Where did you learn them? At school? At home? At club meetings? From peers? Do you still sing these songs today? What memories do they evoke?

SUGGESTIONS FOR PROJECTS

1. Observe a group time in a preschool. Did it include singing? Observe a group time in kindergarten. Did it include singing? Speculate on any differences you found between the two settings.
2. From the bibliography of children's literature in the appendix, select a book that is a picture story of a song. Try reading the book with a group of children. Next, having followed the guidelines for teachers who wish to become song leaders, sing the story. Was there a difference in the interests of the children? Was it possible to initiate a group sing-along?
3. Teach a song that is currently popular to a group of intermediate-grade children. Improvise some simple actions to go with it. Afterward, informally survey the children. Did they enjoy the song? Do they do much singing in their regular classroom? Would they like to do more singing? Why or why not?

REFERENCES

Andress, B. (1985). The practitioner involves young children in music. In J. Boswell (Ed.), *The young child and music: Contemporary principles in child development and music education* (pp. 53–63). Reston, VA: Music Educators National Conference.

Alper, C. (1987). Early childhood music education. In C. Seefeldt (Ed.), *The early childhood curriculum: A review of current research* (pp. 211–236). New York: Teachers College Press.

Barclay, K. D., & Walwer, L. (1992). Linking lyrics and literacy through song picture books. *Young Children, 47,* 76–85.

Cockburn, V. (1991). The uses of folk music and songwriting in the classroom. *Harvard Educational Review, 61,* 71–79.

Cole, J., & Calmenson, S. (1991). *The eentsy, weentsy spider: Fingerplays and action rhymes.* New York: Mulberry Book.

Davidson, L., McKernon, P., & Gardner, H. (1981). The acquisition of song: A developmental approach. In P. Lehman (Ed.), *Documentary report of the Ann Arbor Symposium.* Reston, VA: Music Educators National Conference.

Delacre, L. (1989). *Arroz con leche: Popular songs and rhymes from Latin America.* New York: Scholastic.

Durrell, A. (1989). *The Diane Goode book of American folk tales and songs.* New York: Dutton Child Books.

Gardner, H. (1981, December). Do babies sing a universal song? *Psychology Today,* 70–76.

Gardner, H. (1983). *Frames of mind.* New York: Basic Books.

Gardner, H. (1989). Balancing specialized and comprehensive knowledge: The growing educational challenge. In T. Sergiovani & J. Moore (Eds.), *Schooling for tomorrow: Directing reform to issues that count* (pp. 148–165). Boston: Allyn & Bacon.

Glazer, T. (1990). *The Mother Goose songbook.* New York: Doubleday.

Graham, C. R. (1985). Music and the learning of language in early childhood. In J. Bosell (Ed.), *The young child and music: Contemporary principles in child development and music education* (pp. 109–110). Reston, VA: Music Educators National Conference.

Hammer, R. (1978). *Singing: An extension of speech.* Metuchen, NJ: Scarecrow Press.

Hart, J. (1992). *Singing bee! A collection of favorite children's songs.* New York: Lothrop.

Haywood, C. (1966). *Folk songs of the world.* New York: John Day.

Holahan, J. J. (1985). The development of music syntax: Some observations of music babble in young children. In J. Boswell (Ed.), *The young child and music: Contemporary principles in child development and music education* (pp. 111–112). Reston, VA: Music Educators National Conference.

Jalongo, M. R., & Bromley, K. D. (1984). Developing linguistic competence through song picture books. *The Reading Teacher, 37,* 840–845.

Jalongo, M. R., & Collins, M. (1985). Singing with young children. *Young Children, 40,* 17–22.

Jenkins, E. (1966). *Songbook for children.* New York: Oak Publications.

Lamme, L. L. (1979). Song picture books: A maturing genre of children's literature. *Language Arts, 56,* 400–407.

Lamme, L. L. (1990). Exploring the world of music through picture books. *The Reading Teacher, 44,* 294–301.

Lauritzen, P. (1982). *Preschool song kit.* Rio Vista, CA: Ways and Means Curriculum.

McCracken, R., & McCracken, M. (1986). *Stories, songs, and poetry to teach reading and writing.* Chicago: American Library Association.

McDonald, D. (1979). *Music in our lives: The early years.* Washington, DC: National Association for the Education of Young Children.

Miller, L. (1987). Children's musical behavior in the natural environment. In J. C. Peery, I. W. Peery, & T. W. Draper (Eds.), *Music and child development* (pp. 206–224). New York: Springer-Verlag.

National Gallery of Art (1991). *An illustrated treasury of songs: Traditional American songs, ballads, folk songs, nursery rhymes.* New York: Rizzoli.

Seeger, R. (1980). *Folk songs for children.* Garden City, NY: Doubleday.

Weil, L. (1989). *The magic of music.* New York: Holiday House.

CHAPTER 9

Photography: An Alternative Way of Seeing

Enrique exclaims, "It's coming! *Ha venido*!" This intense enthusiasm is evoked not by the arrival of a circus parade, but rather by the gradual construction on light-sensitive film of a picture of Enrique's friend MariaLuisa. Enrique has just taken the portrait with an automatic autofocus camera and together Enrique and MariaLuisa watch the magical appearance of the product of their joint effort. Enrique has assumed the role of portrait photographer; MariaLuisa is a person important enough to be the subject of the photograph. They eagerly race to show and tell their friends and their teacher what they have done. Their photograph will eventually be included in a cooperative class book including both biographies and/or autobiographies and positive peer comments of every member of the class. Photography's potential for such involved self-enhancing projects and paths to literacy will be explored in this chapter.

ENHANCING VISUAL-SPATIAL INTELLIGENCE THROUGH THE USE OF PHOTOGRAPHY

Spatial intelligence is one of Howard Gardner's seven intelligences (1983), one that consists of a broad amalgam of abilities capable of being used in a variety of different arenas. Central to spatial intelligence is the capacity to perceive the visual world accurately (visual-spatial intelligence). Photographs have the unique capacity to document the world visually and to facilitate visual-spatial awareness and also literacy when oral and written perceptions, reflections, and activities are embedded in the photographic experience.

For all children, including children speaking a language other than that of the dominant culture, special needs children, and so-called typical children, photography can be an exciting and gratifying experience. The fact that photographs produce instant results without the more prolonged process of producing a painting or drawing may make photography a more accessible medium than other art forms for children with differing attention spans and differing spectrums of abilities, such as limited drawing skills or lack of fine motor coordination.

Furthermore, because photography differs from drawing and painting in the thinking processes involved, it may appeal to children with different cognitive styles. Painting is an additive process that starts with a blank sheet of paper or canvas upon which, once an idea has been formulated, art materials are added to produce the whole: a painting. On the other hand, photography involves a selective process that begins with decisions concerning what in the world to photograph and proceeds to the techniques to use to accomplish the desired effect (Barrett, 1986). Not only are the processes different; the products are different. Paintings may depict imaginary worlds; photographs depict reality. Photography is a distinct art form with the potential to engage children in meaningful interactions with their world and facilitate the growth of visual-spatial intelligence and literacy.

Photography promotes a new awareness of the world—an alternative way of seeing. Everyday happenings and environments are observed and contemplated with a reflective eye, and soon an inner voice can be heard saying, "That would make a great photograph!" Forms, colors, shapes, light, relationships, perspectives, patterns, composition, and design become focused objects of thought (Palermo, 1988). Photography is a vibrant form of communication that captures and preserves a visual record of a microcosm of reality. If, as Rudolf Arnheim (1969) argues in *Visual Thinking*, our visual perception of the world undergirds our cognitive processes, then visual literacy and the enlightened eye are substantial life-long contributions to both intelligence and an aesthetic enjoyment of the universe.

IDEAS FOR CLASSROOM PRACTICE

Get Ready

For the teacher who wishes to implement the use of photography in a classroom, obtaining cameras is a necessary first step (Waller, 1981). Determine the budget by deciding the type of equipment needed. Automatic cameras are often the best choice for novice photographers because students can concentrate on learning to see rather than getting mired in technical details. Since students work best in pairs, five cameras would be sufficient for a class of 30 children, thus allowing 10 students, or one-third of the class, to work with photographic equipment at one time. More cameras would be desirable if the cost is not prohibitive. Having determined the budget, check with the principal on the feasibility of the project and the possibility of internal or external funding. External funding might include requesting donations from camera shops, fund-raising by parents, or participating in promotional programs by camera manufacturers such as those sponsored by Polaroid (see reference list for more information).

Get Set

After obtaining the cameras, structuring their use comes next. Use a whole class meeting to discuss the project and cover the following information:

1. Provide each student with a diagram labeling the essential parts of a camera (the viewfinder, the lens, and the shutter release button) and with instructions for using the camera that have been adapted from the manufacturer's booklet but rewritten to the comprehension level of the students.
2. Demonstrate the operation of the camera. Include suggestions on holding the camera steady, standing firmly with arms close to the body, and pressing the shutter release gently. Have the class mime taking a picture.
3. Establish rules for check-out and care of the equipment. A log book can be used for check-out and check-in with name, time, camera number, and number of film exposures recorded. (Limit the number of photos each child takes because preplanning is a part of any project; it also keeps the cost of film within budget.) Cameras should be returned to storage in their designated cases or boxes.

4. Provide each student with a pocket folder for handouts, a journal to record experiences during each photographic session, and a portfolio or album to store and/or display photos.
5. Explain to the students that they will work in pairs for photography sessions because working together not only helps when learning something new, but also provides opportunities to solve problems jointly, analyze and reflect on the results orally, and share triumphs. (The teacher's sensitive pairing of the children is critical. Factors to be considered include the children's native language, personalities, and level of abilities.)

A Caveat, Then Go

The fact that making pictures with a camera is an easy process should not obscure the fact that making a good photograph is not (Barrett, 1986). The best way to learn about photography is to take pictures (Laycock, 1979). However, this does not imply a laissez-faire attitude on the part of the teacher but rather the use of projects and assignments to develop a photographer's vision. Although the initial stimuli may come from the teacher, the children should be left alone to provide their own responses. When children have choices, they become involved and identify with their experiences. Viktor Lowenfeld, the renowned art educator, observed that when children create something on their own, they easily speak and write authentically about their work (Michael, 1986). Photography under these circumstances can be one of the most self-motivating paths to literacy.

LEARNING BASIC TECHNIQUES TO PROMOTE PHOTOGRAPHIC COMPETENCE

For children beginning to use a camera, the following tips will lead to better photographs.

1. Find something that interests you to photograph.
2. Get close enough (between 4 and 10 feet).
3. Be sure there is plenty of light.
4. Check the composition and design in the viewfinder.
5. Keep the background simple.
6. Hold the camera steady.
7. Press the shutter release gently.

Simple assignments that elaborate on some of these principles and promote the photographic competence necessary for later work on student-chosen, teacher-facilitated projects are presented below. The students work with partners, with each child taking a turn with the camera. This partnership maximizes the learning and communication involved in completing the assignments and stimulates critical thinking and problem-solving skills. Some examples of such assignments follow.

Assignment Card #1: Distance from Subject

Take two photographs of the same subject. You decide who or what the subject will be. For one photograph stand about 30 feet away from the subject; for the other photograph come in closer to about 4–10 feet. You and your partner decide how to measure the distance. Once each of you has completed your two pictures, discuss which photos were the most interesting and why.

The examples in Figure 9.1 by two 8-year-old photographers show their results in completing the above assignment. A transcript of the dialogue that ensued between the partners Jamal and Devon, two third graders, follows.

DEVON: There's really no comparison. In the first one you can see more stuff in the background, but nobody would ever know what was in the chair if they hadn't taken the picture.

JAMAL: Yeah. I really like the second one. I can see the details of all three of the toys. I like the way we arranged them, but I wish we had used a different colored chair. My doll's clothes and the chair are the same color, and it all blends in. So it looks even worse in the distance picture. You don't know what's going on at *all*.

FIGURE 9.1   Assignment #1: Distance from subject

Assignment Card # 2: Composition

Good composition means that the elements of a picture are organized in an interesting, harmonious manner. Elements such as colors, lines, shapes, shadows, light areas, and the position of your subject contribute to the balance of a good composition. The most boring place to position your subject is in the very center of the picture. Artists use a guideline called the Rule of Thirds in which they mentally divide a picture into thirds by drawing two lines vertically and two horizontally so that the space is divided into nine equal parts. The Rule of Thirds states: "Position the important element in your picture a third of the way from either side and a third of the way from the top or bottom." See the X's on the following diagram:

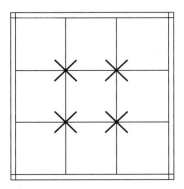

Take two pictures of the same subject. In one, position the subject in your viewfinder exactly in the center and take your picture; in the other picture, utilize The Rule of Thirds and position the subject at one of the intersections of your imaginary horizontal and vertical lines. After each of you has had your turn and the results are printed, discuss which photos you each like and why.

The reviews of the photographs upon completion of the second assignment (see Figure 9.2) were mixed, as the following transcript shows. As a follow-up, the teacher might ask how the direction the doll was facing (toward the side of the picture) influenced the composition.

DEVON: I like the one best where the bear is more in the intersection, like we learned. It's a more interesting picture. When the thing you are photographing is right in the center it looks too fake, like you couldn't think of a better way to do it.

JAMAL: I like the bear looking right straight at me. It's supposed to be boring that way, but I like it better.

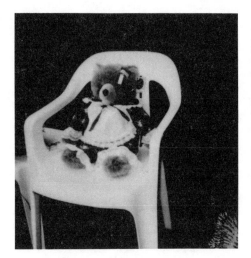 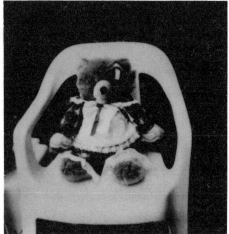

FIGURE 9.2   Assignment #2: Composition

Assignment Card # 3: Light

When you are outdoors, does the position of the sun make a difference in how your picture turns out? Take a picture of your partner with the sun behind you (front lighting). Take another picture with the sun behind your partner (back lighting). Take a third picture with the sun shining on only one side of your partner's face (side lighting). When both of you have completed the assignment, look at the pictures and decide in which picture does the subject squint? In which is the person's face too dark? (National 4-H Council, 1980)

The results of Assignment #3 are shown in Figure 9.3.

The children's comments following completion of the assignment are transcribed below. The children hypothesize about variations in lighting and develop plans for future experimentation, but they make no comment about the mailbox that seems to sprout from Jamal's head. This could elicit a recommendation from the teacher to check the background in the viewfinder before taking the photograph.

DEVON: The one with the sun in their eyes was hard to take. They kept putting their hands up over their eyes, and we had to tell them not to—to look natural—and then they squinted. Actually, both of them had their eyes completely shut.

JAMAL: With the back lighting their faces didn't turn out dark like everyone else's did.

FIGURE 9.3   Assignment #3: Light

DEVON: Yeah, but they have weird light—like a halo—around their hair!

JAMAL: I like the side lighting the best. Except then you get sun on one side of them and shadow on another.

DEVON: And the one little girl was squinting in that one, too.

JAMAL: We should try it at different times in the day when our shadows are long or short and see if it makes any difference.

DEVON: When it's noon and the sun is straight up there in the sky it wouldn't be in their eyes and they wouldn't squint. Let's do that.

Assignment #4: Content

A most important question arises whenever you decide to take a photograph: "What in the world shall I take a picture of?" The answer is "Whatever interests you." Photography reflects the thinking and feeling of the person behind the camera. There are four major categories of subjects for photographs: people, things, places, and happenings. Discuss with your partner which category appeals to you and take two different photos in that category. When both of you have completed the assignment, share your feelings regarding the results.

The photographers took pictures at a birthday party that they both attended. The results are shown in Figure 9.4.

The dialogue that followed completion of this assignment demonstrates a sophisticated awareness of the purpose of photography: communication.

DEVON: I like both of the pictures. I like the way the light shines in Chrissy's hair.

JAMAL: Me, too. But in the first picture I don't know how she's feeling about what she's doing. She was opening a present, I think. The second one I can tell that she likes it.

DEVON: The other children are trying to see what it is, too. They look interested.

The above assignments engage the children in authentic dialogue and problem solving while it increases their awareness of some of the components of photo-

FIGURE 9.4 Assignment #4: Content

graphic literacy. Following the discussions, entries are recorded in a journal to promote the summarizing of experiences, reflective thinking, and also writing skills. The photographs are mounted, dated, identified with pertinent information, perhaps given titles, and stored in a portfolio or photo album for future enjoyment and for the documentation of increasing competency.

USING PHOTOGRAPHY AS A PATH TO LITERACY

The development of photographic skills opens up increasingly expanded opportunities to engage in meaningful projects executed either by an individual or by cooperative groups. The choices and planning of activities involving photographs offer many chances for authentic literacy experiences: reading directions for the use of cameras; maintaining log books of equipment use; writing reflective journals; collaborating and dialoguing with peers; titling and describing photographs; and articulating reasons for liking or disliking photographic works (including the students' own photographs, selections from books that depict photographic collections, or visits to gallery shows). The outcomes of various projects might include individual or cooperative class books, individual portfolios of the students' own photographic work, collaborative photographic exhibitions that include selections by students of representative photographs from their portfolios, show-and-tell presentations to the class of favorite professional photographs, or bulletin board displays of personally selected examples of photographs used in advertising that give background information and state reasons for their appeal.

The selection of a project must reflect the genuine interest of the students and thus result in active participation and engagement in planning, executing, evaluating, and learning. Gardner (1990) in his ARTS PROPEL program speaks of children having the opportunity to produce, perceive, and reflect. He maintains that students throughout a project should look at what they are doing and how they are developing their competencies. In a photographic project Gardner's guidelines are uniquely fulfilled through the opportunity for dialogues, the use of a student-maintained portfolio of photographs, and a written journal. These components encourage literacy and effectively facilitate habits of working, self-initiated assessment, and self-sustained learning (Tchudi, 1991; Zessoules & Gardner, 1991).

A group of enthusiastic photographers might decide to put together an exhibition to share their creations with an audience. The project would involve students in selecting their favorite photos from their portfolios, mounting them attractively, arranging the photographs in aesthetically pleasing ways, titling the works, writing items for a program, and developing announcements of the time and place of the exhibition. All of these activities involve authentic literacy experiences and intrinsically motivated learning. In order to select their favorite photos, students are required to look through their portfolios or albums. This selection process in itself promotes new insights and could promote a crystallizing experience (Gardner, 1990). Students follow their progress to a more advanced level. They step back, decenter, and consider their work reflectively, drawing new insights and ideas about the process of learning. The continuous record promotes concepts of the construction of competence rather than evaluative judgments of good/bad or right/wrong (DeVries & Kohlberg, 1990).

Photographs can provide the stimulus for books and, conversely, books can provide the stimulus for photographs. Groups can choose a theme for a book (for example, the seasons) and create an integrated cooperative book including all of the arts: poetry, photography, painting, written songs (a different symbol system), and written narratives. A documentary on a particular subject, such as Washington Elementary School, can be an individual or a group project. Individual photos of class members can be combined with written autobiographies and positive comments from classmates to create a class yearbook. The opening vignette for this chapter conveys some of the enthusiasm and the involvement that such a project can generate.

Books of photographs develop an appreciation of this visual art form and provide an opportunity to look at and respond to their impact emotionally, verbally, and in written form. Outstanding, brilliant collections of photographs are available at bookstores and libraries. Some examples are *Ansel Adams: The Eloquence of Light* (Booth-Clibborn, 1983), *The Art of Color Photography* (Hedgecoe, 1978), *Images of the World* (National Geographic, 1981), *Patterns in Nature* (Schneck, 1991), and *Sports People* (Iooss, 1988). (See also the bibliography of children's literature in the appendix for children's books with photographs as illustrations.) The probability of finding a book that intrigues a student is very high. Looking through a book just for pleasure, to select a favorite for a show-and-tell session, or to analyze in writing the effectiveness of a particular photograph expands awareness of the potential of the camera and promotes opportunities for the development and use of literary skills.

Laura Chapman (1978) has stated that a well-developed sense of perception is necessary for creating expressive works of art. Creating some criteria for evaluating photographs of others can also lead to self-evaluation of one's own efforts. A simple open-ended checklist such as the one included in this chapter's appendix could be used to foster awareness of the elements of a photograph that enhance its visual and affective impact: "What makes one photograph powerful and riveting while another seems dull and uninteresting?"

Photography is an intriguing art form that captures children's interests and imaginations, invites their responses, and requires easily mastered competencies. Through photographic projects children become involved in their own self-motivated education (Schwartz, 1988). They realize they *can* learn something new, they *can* do things that are worthwhile and that command respect. These realizations nourish feelings of self-worth and dispositions to learn—to learn photography and to learn to read, to write, and to communicate with others. The mind-set might well be contagious.

SUMMARY

Photography as an exciting child-compatible art form promotes visual-spatial intelligence and new awareness of the world, and also provides an alternative path to activities that promote literacy. For the teacher who wishes to use photography in the classroom, obtaining the necessary equipment and instructing the students in its proper care and use are precursors to the development of photographic skills. Working in pairs, students complete assignments collaboratively, maintain individual portfolios, and engage in reflective journal writing. Once students have acquired photographic competency, the opportunities for projects in which authentic literacy experiences are embedded expand to include individual and cooperative class books, collaborative exhibitions, and evaluation of one's own photographs and those in books and museums by using a suggested review form.

QUESTIONS FOR JOURNAL WRITING AND DISCUSSION

1. Does your family have a photo album? If so, look through the album and select a photograph that particularly appeals to you. Why do you think you selected the photograph?
2. What advantages and disadvantages do you see with portfolio assessment as compared with a more formal form of assessment such as tests? Does this type of assessment meet the needs of the student? The teacher? The parent of the student? An administrator?
3. What experiences have you had with photography? How could photography lead to growth in visual-spatial intelligence? Do you agree with Arnheim's statement that "our visual perception of the world undergirds our cognitive processes." In what way?

SUGGESTIONS FOR PROJECTS

1. First, from a collection of photographs in a book or a museum or gallery show of photography, select one photograph and use the evaluation sheet to record your reactions to and feelings about it. Then, take a photograph yourself and again use the evaluation sheet to record your reactions to and feelings about your photograph. Did using the evaluation sheet lead to insights into your own photographic techniques?
2. Select a child aged 8 or above who has not had any experience with a camera. Explain the basics of using a camera, following the tips listed in the chapter. Have the child complete two of the four assignment cards. What was the child's reaction? Did he or she wish to continue and complete the rest of the assignments?
3. From the library, select a book of photographs that have been taken by a nationally acclaimed or world-renowned photographer. In your opinion, what makes this person a "great" photographer? How does this photographer demonstrate his or her knowledge of basic photographic techniques, such as distance from subject, content, light, and composition? How do you think this photographer demonstrates visual-spatial intelligence?

REFERENCES

Arnheim, R. (1969). *Visual thinking.* Berkeley: University of California Press.
Barrett, T. (1986). Teaching about photography. *Art Education, 39,* 12–15.
Booth-Clibborn, E. (1983). *Ansel Adams: The eloquence of light.* New York: Aperture.

Chapman, L. (1978). *Approaches to art in education*. San Diego: Harcourt Brace Jovanovich.

DeVries, R., & Kohlberg, L. (1990). *Constructivist early education: Overview and comparison with other programs*. Washington, DC: National Association for the Education of Young Children.

Gardner, H. (1983). *Frames of mind*. New York: Basic Books.

Gardner, H. (1990). Multiple intelligences: Implications for art and creativity in W. J. Moody (Ed.), *Artistic intelligences: Implications for education*. New York: Teachers College Press, 11–27.

Hedgecoe, J. (1978). *The art of color photography*. New York: Simon & Schuster.

Iooss, W. (1988). *Sports people*. New York: Harry Abrams.

Laycock, G. (1979). *The complete beginner's guide to photography*. Garden City, NY: Doubleday.

Michael, J. (1986). Viktor Lowenfeld: Some misconceptions, some insights. *Art Education, 39*, 36–39.

National 4-H Council (1980). *Adventures with your camera*. Washington, DC: Author.

National Geographic (1981). *Images of the world*. Washington, DC: Author.

Palermo, P. (1988). Photography: A diary for life. *Arts and Activities, 103*, 38–39.

Polaroid Education Program, for information write 28 Osborn Street, Cambridge, MA 02139, or phone (617) 577-5090.

Schneck, M. (1991). *Patterns in nature*. New York: Crescent Books.

Schwartz, B. (1988). Photography and self-image. *Arts and Activities, 44*, 24–25.

Tchudi, S. (1991). *Planning and assessing the curriculum in English language arts*. Alexandria, VA: Association for Supervision and Curriculum Development.

Waller, V. (1981). Lights, camera, action! The camera as a tool for teaching reading. In Alfred Ciani (Ed.), *Motivating reluctant readers*. Newark, DE: International Reading Association.

Zessoules, R., & Gardner, H. (1991). Authentic assessment: Beyond the buzzword and into the classroom. In V. Perrone (Ed.), *Expanding student assessment* (pp. 47–71). Alexandria, VA: Association for Supervision and Curriculum Development.

APPENDIX

My Reactions to and Feelings about a Photograph

Name _____

Date _____

1. *Title of the Photograph*:

- Does the photograph have a title? If it does, write it down.
- If the photograph does not have a title or you would like another one better, write your original title here.

2. *Source*:

- If the photograph comes from a magazine or book, write the page number and the exact title of the book or magazine.
- If this is one of your photographs, provide information on when you took the photograph, and why you selected this subject.
- If the photograph was taken by someone else or you saw the photograph at a museum or gallery show, give as much information as you want about the photographer or your trip to the museum or gallery, its location, and your reaction to the experience.

3. *Personal Reactions to and Feelings about the Photograph*:

- Photographer's Purpose: What message was the photographer trying to communicate?
- Use of Color: What colors were used, and how did they affect you?
- Lighting: What type of lighting was used, and how did it affect you?
- Composition: What about the placement of the people and objects in space?
- Personal Meaning: Does the photograph remind you of something in your own life? Write about it.

CHAPTER 10

Dance: The Most Ancient of Arts

Several years ago one of the authors had the exciting opportunity to teach a class of West Indian children on the Caribbean island of St. Croix. One day it was decided to turn *Hansel and Gretel*, one of the children's favorite folk tales, into a three-act play. The children inexplicably resisted modifying the text into their pleasantly lilting dialect, so the author was dismayed at the resulting stilted nature of their interpretation of the story. The European syntax and story grammar had little significance to their own experience; it seemed clear that while they enjoyed reading the story, they were somewhat uncomfortable with its oral interpretation.

On a whim, the author brought in some reggae music that was popular at that time in an attempt to perhaps make the play more "cross-cultural." The results were astounding. The children, with very little input, immediately began moving their bodies to the music, acting out their individual reactions to their first encounter with the wicked witch in abrupt, angular motions. They then shoved the witch into the oven with one broad staccato movement, finally expressing their glee at the death of the witch with flying, leaping motions. The witch was dead, but the story had suddenly come to life! The story had now actually cut across cultures and had clearly been internalized by the children in the most personal and profound way.

Through the above experience the author began to see the infinite possibilities of using dance with children as a potent means of self-expression and a vehicle through which they might construct meaning from literature. Dance could be a "natural" part of any literacy program, for long before words are used, aren't children already competent at communicating meanings through movement? Though these early motions are often purely functional, consciously ordered motion—or "dance"—can be used to express a child's every emotional state (California State Board of Education, 1989). It follows logically, then, that children can also learn to convey those same emotions as they are encountered in literature.

The remainder of this chapter addresses the potential for using dance forms to enrich and extend reading and writing and thinking in elementary classrooms.

COMMUNICATION THROUGH DANCE

World-famous dancer Isadora Duncan is credited as having said, "If I could *tell* you what I mean, there would be no point in dancing!" Her somewhat facetious statement underscores the communicative nature of dance; there are simply times when feelings, emotions, and ideas that are culturally patterned can only be expressed through body movements, or in pop psychology jargon, "body language." Nonverbal body movements, as compared with ordinary motor activities, can become vehicles of conceptualization, harbingers of very personal messages, or even conveyers of cultural traditions and ideas.

Just as in oral and written language, the communication of feelings and thoughts through symbols is an essential ingredient of dance. The symbols used are accessible to all ages, for they, like language, may be basic and realistic or complex and abstract. Some dance movements can have universally shared meanings, such as jumping for joy, cowering in fear, withdrawing in sorrow, approaching, fleeing, or attacking.

However, the meaning of most dance movements is rich in cultural ideas, as when Maori warriors extend their tongues to express, in their culture, power and dominance. It is also important to note that the symbols portrayed by the dance may be significant even when the dancer has no such meaning in mind, as when a dancer creates a dance full of frenetic energy that, in another culture, connotes a mating call. In other cases, the spectators, taking an active role in receiving the symbolic communication, construe their own personal, idiosyncratic associations and meanings to the visual images presented by the dancers.

The ability to symbolize through dance, as in language, extends the child's knowledge of the world and its ways. Whatever else dance may be, its strong interface between motor and cognitive activities makes it a unique way of receiving and expressing knowledge. J. L. Hanna (1983) describes the connection between dance and "knowing" in the following way: "When there is no link between thinking, feeling, and doing, there is no self-control. Without this, there is no dance."

A RATIONALE FOR INTEGRATING DANCE AND LITERACY

Of all the arts that are given even the most superficial placement in American elementary classrooms, dance and creative movement have probably received the least amount of attention. For those children with parents unable to afford lessons at private dance studios, exposure to dance in the early years is especially meager, generally consisting of the children being subjugated to the role of audience at an amateur performance or two. While in many cultures dance is an integral part of religious customs and rituals, it has no such place of significance in American culture. How, then, can an alliance of dance and literacy be rationalized by teachers who must keep a constant vigil of accountability for their curricular choices? As an answer, these points culled from *Dance as Education* (Fowler, 1978) are offered for consideration:

- Exposure to dance—both as spectators and participants—helps children to understand and appreciate their own culture and the cultures of others, as illustrated by the example of West Indian children in this chapter's introduction.
- The basic components of dance—pattern, line, form, shape, time, rhythm, and energy—are pivotal concepts in many other curricular areas and can therefore be integrated with and enhance mathematics and the social sciences, as well as the language arts.
- Dance provides an intuitive, affective mode of knowing through kinesthetic expression. Moreover, the activities of improvising and combining patterns of movement help children to discover their ability to create spontaneously.
- Finally, including dance as an avenue of self-expression affords an alternative way of being successful for ESL learners and other children

who do not or cannot respond successfully to verbal instruction, as well as for those children whose primary orientation is physical rather than mental.

IDEAS FOR CLASSROOM PRACTICE

To best understand how literacy and dance can be integrated into a whole-language classroom, let us look at the activities in a fourth-grade classroom in the San Juan Unified School District, where a grant from the Getty Foundation has enabled selected teachers to discover ways of merging literacy and the arts. In this exemplary classroom, Karla Cheevey, who has dabbled in ballet and tap dancing over the years, teaches reading and writing with literature. Karla and her pupils engage in authentic adventures through a variety of activities that allow children to find their own personal significance in books: they read stories to themselves and/or with reading buddies, they form self-selected literature response groups, the teacher reads aloud to the whole class, and small groups of children choose to retell the stories orally or to reenact them in skit form. The children also express their reactions to literature via their dialogue journals, excerpts of which they select to share in their response groups.

In their response groups, they struggle to understand the content of stories that they have read and to discuss the meaning as it relates to their own lives. What is especially striking to an observer in this classroom is how the children, in their discussions, seem to zero in on the key ideas in the literature. As examples, consider the following excerpts from the children's discussions:

> On *The Bridge to Terabithia* (Paterson, 1977): "Jesse and Leslie were friends in a really special way. The other children couldn't understand that friendship, maybe because they were jealous or maybe because it doesn't happen like that very often between a fifth-grade boy and girl."
>
> On *Tuck Everlasting* (Babbitt, 1975): "I wonder if people really want to live forever, or if they just think they do. I mean, it's like when you think you could never get tired of ice cream and then for your birthday you're allowed to eat all you want and you get so full and sick of it."
>
> On *Summer of the Swans* (Byers, 1980): "I couldn't stand the part where they were searching for Charlie. It was like a scary movie where at any time you expect to find something horrible around the corner. It was a black, cloudy feeling."

After the children have had discussions like the above examples in their response groups, the teacher sets aside time twice a week for the dance workshop. During this hour, the children select one or two key ideas from the story that they would like to express in dance form to enrich the story. Specifically, children are asked to consider three elements of the story that could be expressed creatively through dance: its structure, mood, and symbols or extended metaphors contained in the work (Eeds & Peterson, 1990).

- *Structure:* Children are asked to consider the tension that the author has set up through the events in the story, and how he or she goes about relieving this tension. What point do children consider to be the climax or the most intense event in the story? How would they move their bodies to show this tension?

- *Mood:* Children are asked to examine how they felt at any particular point in the story, or to consider the emotional state of the author of the book. Was there any part of the book that was intensely happy, sad, scary, or moving? How could their bodies move to express these feelings?

- *Symbol or extended metaphors:* Children are asked what is "true" about the story in a way that they may not have thought about before. How does the meaning affect them? What has the author told them about *their* lives? How could their bodies move to these new ideas?

Next, from a selection of classical music that has been played continuously during the week, the children select, by popular vote, the piece they consider most evocative of the feelings set forth in the literature with which they will be working. The class then breaks up into several small groups that will collaborate on original dances to express the themes that the children have culled from the literature. After several sessions of working on their expressive dances, each group then presents its dance to the rest of the class. The whole class shares its feelings as to how the mood, structure, symbols, and other key ideas have been captured through the dance.

The dance is further integrated with the literature and language as the children describe creating their dance, and their feelings about it, in their journals. From these journal entries, excerpts selected by the children may be shared in small groups or with the whole class.

Finally, videotaping the dances allows a new dimension of observation and reflection. Throughout the year, children enjoy seeing their creations "immortalized" on film and can respond to their own growth in expression, while reliving a fondly recalled piece of literature.

SOME POSITIVE OUTCOMES
FROM DANCE WORKSHOPS

A program for creative movement and dance at another school, the Awakening Seed School in Tempe, Arizona (Mersereau, Glover, & Cherland, 1989), uses the imagery and evocative language of poetry to help children visualize images that they then translate into dance forms. For example, one class chose the winter solstice as a theme for writing and dance. The teacher read a collection of autumn and winter poetry to the children and invited the children to brainstorm their ideas and feelings about this time of year. Then they created dances about the winter solstice. The children began to express such a sense of unity between the images of the poetry that was read and the movements in their dances that they spontaneously began writing their *own* poetry, offering to their teachers a graphic insight into the similarities between the composing processes in both written expression and dance.

The children involved in the dance program at Awakening Seed School serendipitously showed their teachers a further impact that dance can have on literacy: children began to see language's ability to enhance the creative process. As they created their dances and practiced them with the intention of presenting them to their classmates, the children found that using language to name discrete motions or routines that had been used allowed them to recall and replicate those actions over time. Thus, a sequence of sharp staccato movements, for example, became known as "chips and dips." Having a specific vocabulary for their dance steps enabled them to create more sophisticated dances.

OTHER CONSIDERATIONS REGARDING DANCE

Though Karla Cheevey and the teachers at the Awakening Seed School have had some formal training in dance, many who are incorporating dance into their literacy programs have had no such exposure. A formal background in dance is simply not necessary. Paul Werner (1990) insists that, while a teacher of dance in an elementary classroom should be enthusiastic about creative movement, he or she need not be concerned that the product is always "artistically pleasing" or "creative." Rather, Werner urges teachers to be more concerned with the entire learning process of creating the dance. Furthermore, he exhorts teachers to encourage children to learn to create dances not by watching others or by direct instruction, but through their own problem solving, discovery, and creative explorations.

SUMMARY

The potential for using dance as an alternative way for children to demonstrate "artful knowing" (Gim, 1989, p. 18) is vast. Children need to learn with their bodies, minds, and hearts, for children may approach learning in varying ways at various times in their lives. Through dance, children can be given the opportunity to internalize and express their understandings of concepts in an original and kinesthetic way. They can use other modes of discourse, such as poetry, to further conceptualize their understandings. Finally, they may discover an empowering new use for language, as they begin to see the need for naming their various expressive movements.

A poem by Seymour Kleinman (1990) sums up the tremendous power unleashed by integrating dance with language:

Words and actions merge,
Becoming deed.
Speech and gesture become one;

The word and the flesh are one:
Mouth and hand,
Torso and head,
Heart and mind,
Breath and soul.
All organs of expression,
Orgasmic, organic pathways,
Wholeness in practice and performance,
All into one:
All are one. (p. 129)

QUESTIONS FOR JOURNAL WRITING AND DISCUSSION

1. What do you think was meant by Isadora Duncan's statement "If I could *tell* you what I mean, there would be no point in dancing!" Describe some feelings, emotions, or ideas that you feel would best be expressed through dance.

2. Why do you think dance has been largely neglected in elementary curricula in the United States? Give a rationale you might present to a school board for including dance in a school in which many nonnative English speakers are enrolled.

3. Discuss the composing process of both written expression and dance. How are they similar? Different? How do your feelings about the nature of the two processes compare with the insights developed by the children at the Awakening Seed School as presented in this chapter?

4. Think back to your own experiences with dance. Have you been more a spectator or a participant? How would you have changed this?

SUGGESTIONS FOR PROJECTS

1. Obtain a video of *Giselle, Rodeo, Swan Lake,* or another ballet with which you are unfamiliar. Try to get a sense of the story that is being presented through the movement of the dancers. Then read the synopsis of the ballet that accompanies the video. Compare your ideas about the story with the actual synopsis. Were you able to get the gist of the story line without any prior knowledge of the ballet? How were the dancers able to convey the story to the audience without words?

2. Select one of your favorite children's stories from your personal library or from the bibliography at the end of this text. Consider the structure, mood, and symbols or metaphors used in the story, as explained in this chapter. Plan how you could express these three elements of the story creatively through body movements. If you wish, share your movement ideas with a small group of fellow students.

3. To further your own understanding of dance, read *Swan Lake* by Margot Fonteyn, which provides a history of ballet as well as many personal anecdotes, including the author's experience dancing the lead.

REFERENCES

Babbitt, N. (1975). *Tuck everlasting*. New York: Farrar, Straus, & Giroux.

Byers, B. (1980). *Summer of the swans*. New York: Viking.

California State Board of Education. (1989). *Visual and performing arts framework.* Sacramento, CA: Author.

Eeds, M., & Peterson, R. (1990). *Grand conversations: Literature groups in action*. New York: Scholastic–TAB.

Fowler, C. R. (1978). *Dance as education*. Washington, DC: American Alliance for Health, Physical Education, Recreation, and Dance.

Gim, J. M. (1989). *Physical education as artful knowing*. Unpublished doctoral dissertation, Ohio State University, Columbus.

Hanna, J. L. (1983). The mentality and matter of dance. *Art Education, 36*(2), 42–46.

Kleinman, S. (1990). Intelligent kinesthetic expression. In W. J. Moody (Ed.), *Artistic intelligences: Implications for education*. New York: Teachers College Press.

Mersereau, Y., Glover, M., & Cherland, M. (1989). Dancing on the edge. *Language Arts, 62,* 109–118.

Paterson, K. (1977). *Bridge to Terabithia*. New York: Crowell.

Werner, P. (1990). Implications for movement. In W. J. Moody (Ed.), *Artistic intelligences: Implications for education*. New York: Teachers College Press.

PART III

Appreciation: Perceiving and Valuing

CHAPTER **11**

Talking and Writing
about Picasso (and Others)

Art has often been considered a mere "frill" in the elementary school curriculum, a once or twice weekly event where children are aproned and armed with paint-brushes or modeling clay. The products are relegated to the refrigerator door or the coffee table, and neither parent nor classroom teacher is quite convinced that there are any real academic outcomes from such a trivial pursuit.

Happily, many philosophical and curricular changes have occurred in art educa-tion that have been initiated by art education and endorsed by the National Art Education Association. A significant change has been a move to expand art education beyond teaching and encouraging self-expression. The more traditional "studio art," which once dominated art instruction in most elementary classrooms, is being cojoined by the sharing of concepts in art history, art criticism, and aesthetics (Eisner, 1987; Dobbs, 1988). This new attitude on the part of art educators is partially in response to a demand for accountability for all components of an overcrowded curriculum; in order to survive, art education must be seen by classroom teachers and parents as much more than isolated, frivolous activity that has little to do with the academic fundamentals. With the additional elements in art education, however, art can now be dynamically integrated with the language arts of speaking and writing.

The concepts of art history, art criticism, and aesthetics can best be shared with children who have been exposed to many works of art and who feel free to talk about their responses in their own unique ways. Children can easily be over-whelmed by art "experts" who use a strange vocabulary and seem to look at the art in a vague and unfamiliar way. One of the authors can best use personal childhood memories as an example of this.

"I have always loved art. Indeed, some of my most vivid memories of childhood center around the musty aroma of city art galleries, where I was often aesthetically excited by the visual array of artwork I discovered there. But I also remember staring silently at the paintings—a sharp contrast to my usual talkative self. Perhaps I was merely in awe. Or maybe I subconsciously feared that I lacked the appropriate words to share my primitive feelings about the many paintings to which I was attracted. While the adults surrounding me freely expressed their unbridled enthusi-asm for 'the interesting use of the palette knife,' 'the texture,' or 'the mood' of certain pieces, I was left to wonder if I really had a right to an opinion about a painting if I could not clearly justify my viewpoint with words that were sufficiently esoteric.

"In retrospect, it seems that my first reaction to the arts was limited by my lack of 'mature' language skills. I know now that it needn't have been so. Teachers can offer intermediate-grade children access to their own visceral reactions to art by merely modeling a wide variety of personal responses, affirming the oral responses of individual children, and in turn giving children plenty of opportunities to discuss and write about art in their own terms. Such lessons open the wonderful world of art to children, but can also become integrated into excellent oral-language activities while encouraging a most original form of descriptive writing and reflective poetry. Additionally, such lessons open children's minds to exposure to the arts as symbolic communication. As the world-famous dancer Rudolf Nureyev explained, concerning the transfer of art to language, 'If you know one subject very well then you have the key to every other subject. If you know one language very well, you know structure, syntax, grammar. With all that, you can quickly assimilate another language' (Lemay, 1990)."

IDEAS FOR CLASSROOM PRACTICE

Selecting Fine Art

A first step in sharing fine art with children is selecting a wide range of paintings to which they can be exposed. It may be best to provide a sampling of several different genres ranging from the stark symbols of Aaron Douglas's *Building More Stately Mansions* or Picasso's simple, linear *Hand with Flowers*, to some of the more flowery Impressionist works such as Monet's *Water Lilies.* Such artwork can be obtained simply and inexpensively from art magazines and from calendars containing suitable works of art, or they can be borrowed from the public library. Even postcards from art galleries, though somewhat smaller, can be matted attractively for this purpose. Next, a different painting can be prominently displayed each day and ceremoniously introduced. The teacher can tell a bit about the artist, his or her life and times, and the title of the piece, while perhaps sharing some personal reactions to the works.

As a further resource, the teacher can get to know the wide range of artists living in the community and invite some of them to share their works with the children. To prevent children from believing that any one artist's genre, methods, and products are the *only* ones, it is critical to seek a variety of presentations—from a Hmong woman sharing how she embroiders a flower cloth to an impressionistic artist or a more realistic Norman Rockwell–type artist whose vision is in portraying scenes exactly as they are. Presentations should be prefaced with the caveat "This artist will show us *one* way to paint (sculpt, draw, etc.). This is how he (or she) sees it and does it." Afterward, children should be encouraged to offer their impression of the artist's work, how it makes them feel, and what it reminds them of, as suggested in the next section.

Responding to the Paintings

When paintings (or drawings, sculpture, etc.) have been introduced, the next step is to encourage children to take a few minutes to study all the paintings while taking notes. Ask them to look at the paintings and think about the following:

"Which painting speaks to you most? What does it say?"

"What aspect of the painting attracts you?"

"What in your own life does the painting remind you of?"

"What are some places, people, and images that the painting brings to your mind?"

"Write down some words and open-ended phrases that express some of the feelings that you have about this painting."

Such broad yet focused questions avoid the implied need for justification inherent in more evaluative questions such as "Which painting do you like best? Why?"

To best illustrate how these questions might be answered, the teacher can demonstrate by selecting a painting that speaks to him or her and musing aloud as to what it is about the work that is appealing and how it relates to his or her life.

Similarly, to focus on one piece of art long enough to build a deeper appreciation and afford a truly memorable experience, a more in-depth discussion can be generated by preparing specific questions for the students, such as the questions below that pertain to the work *Woman and Child Driving*:

Woman and Child Driving *by Mary Cassatt*

What is the first thing you noticed about this painting?

How many people are in the painting?

Where do you think they are going? Why?

What do you think the little girl is thinking about?

Describe the clothes the woman is wearing.

How do the woman and the little girl feel about one another? Why do you think so?

Are the people looking forward to going where they are headed?

Which person in the painting would you most like to be? Why?

What might be a good name for this painting?

Comparing Paintings

When children have had time to reflect upon their feelings and reactions to a painting of their choice, they then search for a partner who has chosen a painting that is very unlike their chosen painting in some respect. For example, one child with a dark painting may decide to team up with another who has chosen a very bright painting; or one child's chosen painting may consist of many animals in motion while the other's contains one lone person sitting quietly.

The two children then sit down together and, using their list of words and phrases, write down in one column some words that express what is similar about the two paintings and, in another column, what is different about them. The teacher can instruct them to use a Venn diagram, as in Figure 11.1, to illustrate graphically their comparative ideas and to show how the paintings are similar and dissimilar.

The pair of children may then use their Venn diagram as a "prop" to discuss the paintings they have selected with the rest of the class. This sharing will most likely be for many the most enjoyable—if not the first—art commentary they have ever experienced.

As an alternative activity, each child may slowly read all of his or her words and phrases that were inspired by the chosen painting. The child then encourages the

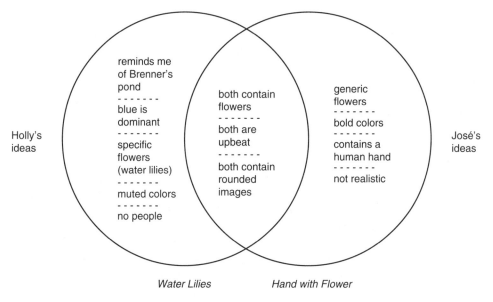

Holly's ideas

reminds me of Brenner's pond
- - - - - -
blue is dominant
- - - - - -
specific flowers (water lilies)
- - - - - -
muted colors
- - - - - -
no people

both contain flowers
- - - - - -
both are upbeat
- - - - - -
both contain rounded images

generic flowers
- - - - - -
bold colors
- - - - - -
contains a human hand
- - - - - -
not realistic

José's ideas

Water Lilies   *Hand with Flower*

FIGURE 11.1 Venn diagram

other class members to guess which painting is being described and to tell exactly which words or phrases led them to their conclusion.

A contrast frame is an excellent vehicle through which the children may now extend their responses to their chosen paintings into the writing realm. The Venn diagram will have already helped them to graphically see the similarities and differences between their two chosen paintings; the contrast frame will further allow children to organize their thinking about the paintings, while helping them to establish a schema for writing about art (Cudd, 1990).

The Venn diagram in Figure 11.1, converted into a contrast frame, might look like Figure 11.2.

FIGURE 11.2 Contrast frame

Contrast frame

Water Lilies and *Hand with Flowers* differ in several ways.

First, *Water Lilies* is _____

while *Hand with Flowers* is _____

Second, *Water Lilies* is _____

while *Hand with Flowers* is _____

Probably the way the two paintings are the most different is that _____

_____

_____

Poetry Inspired by Art

It should not be surprising to discover that the words, phrases, and images that children use to describe how their painting "speaks" to them may be the very ingredient of which fresh, reflective poetry is made. In many cases, children will have independently made this discovery themselves and will have already gone on to put their feelings and responses to the artwork into free verse poetry. Other children can make the connection to poetry with the help of a simple structure that lends itself to poetic ideas, such as in Figure 11.3. To use this structure, the teacher asks children to take their words, phrases, and images and place them into the blanks, adding various articles (*the, an, a*) or prepositions (*onto, through, above*) as desired. Children should be encouraged to experiment with the placement of words into the blanks until they have created a poem that "feels right" to them. If they wish, children can consult trusted friends for second opinions about the best placements for their words and phrases.

In the example of Monet's *Water Lilies*, used for the Venn diagram and contrast frame described previously, the words and phrases expressed by the child who selected this painting might be arranged as poetry as in Figure 11.4.

The Illustrator's Art

Beside classical artists, the work of various illustrators of children's picture storybooks, such as Leo Lionni, Ezra Jack Keats, or Chris Van Allsburg, can be a source of aesthetic appreciation in the elementary classroom. Each week teachers can introduce a new illustrator of children's books. Children can compare the different styles of art used in various books illustrated by one illustrator. Children will conclude, with guidance, that an illustrator uses a very distinctive style consistently that they will soon begin to recognize. Genuine appreciation follows with this familiarity.

Children can also be led to appreciate how certain illustrations add richly to favorite stories. For example, in Leo Lionni's *Inch by Inch* the use of collage provides textures that appear to add a third dimension to the story; similarly, the pictures in *Once a Mouse . . .* not only complete the brief text, but add a perspective of their own.

Illustrations also play a significant part in how the reader responds to a story. To

FIGURE 11.3 Poetry structure

Poetry structure

Water Lilies: A Reaction

Like Brenner's Pond,
Full of color.
Lilies.
So many flowers!
Springtime.
Blue dominates.   **FIGURE 11.4**

emphasize this point, several versions of familiar stories illustrated by different artists can be shared with children, such as *Cinderella* or *Little Red Riding Hood*. In small share groups, the children can discuss their feelings about the illustrator's style, use of colors, and the mood that was created, or anything else that occurs to them about the pictures in the book. In their own words, they can tell what they think the illustrator was trying to do by designing the pictures the way he or she did. Spokespersons for each group can compare the group's feelings about their illustrator's work with the responses elicited from other groups toward their illustrator's work. The teacher can then reflect upon which illustrations the children prefer and why.

SHARING THE TERMINOLOGY OF PAINTING

Children must always feel free to respond to paintings and other art forms using their own words, feelings, and ideas. It is critical to send the message that there is no one "right" response. As mentioned earlier, nothing "turns children off" more quickly than believing themselves to be too unsophisticated in their knowledge of artistic terminology to merit an opinion. However, children can be introduced to some of the vocabulary that artists use in developmentally appropriate and non-threatening ways by a teacher who models the terms using a think-aloud strategy while talking about the paintings. For example, the following terms if shared with children will offer them a more precise way to crystallize their own ideas (Warner, 1989):

Painting Words to Use with Primary Children
Paint
    tempera paint, watercolor paint
    thick paint, thin paint
    drips, drops
Brushes, Strokes
    wide brush, narrow brush
    hard bristles, soft bristles
    long stroke, short stroke, curved stroke
    dot, dab
Color
    light, dark

bright, dull
mix colors, blend colors
Shape
big shape, small shape (p. 36)

Painting Words to Use with Intermediate Children
Paint
tempera = opaque
watercolor = transparent
tint, shade
Color
related colors
monochromatic
value = light and dark
Composition
pattern
scale
overlap
Printmaking
monoprint, stamp print
reversed image
raised surface, etched surface (p. 158)

INTEGRATING THE VISUAL ARTS

In the most profound sense, not only can the entire range of content area in an elementary curriculum be used to make children aware of the importance of art to the entire curriculum, but concepts can be made clearer through the visual image. For example, children can be exposed to ideas from the French Revolution by presenting to them the paintings of Jean Honoré Fragonard and Jaques Louis David, while a unit on French customs and food can be enhanced through the introduction of still life paintings by Jean Baptiste Siméon Chardin. Similarly, important lessons in ecology and the environment can be underscored and brought to life by showing children photographs of the erosion of the magnificent architectural monuments in Greece and Italy (Godfrey, 1992).

Also, teachers can make graphic statements to children about the value of diverse cultures and the equity of genders, races, and lifestyles by introducing children not only to the creative works of Anglo males, but additionally to a wide assortment of works by people of color, women, and artists who are living or have led various lifestyles. By a deliberate attempt on the part of the teacher not to evaluate artists but to allow children to respond to the works in their own ways, as described in this chapter, children will begin to appreciate a constellation of artistic works that reflect a variety of cultures and experiences.

Finally, artists can be "brought to life" in a literary sense through their biographies. To further understanding of the historical context of paintings and the range of emotions connected with the artists' lives, biographies of artists can be shared with children. New insights and connections with the artist are made possible. For example, children who are attracted to Mary Cassatt's vivid Japanese-inspired portraits of mothers and children often find the biography *Mary Cassatt* (Cain, 1989) fascinating. Though now generally regarded as one of the finest painters of the Impressionist era, Mary Cassatt was discouraged by her father—and society in general—from pursuing a career in art. Such a pursuit was at odds with the time and expectations for a woman of her class. Yet high-spirited Mary Cassatt persevered and through her prolific career changed society's views about art and women. This historically based story can offer children a new appreciation not only of the artist, but of how her ideas and paintings evolved.

SUMMARY

Art appreciation can be integrated with oral and written language by allowing children to respond to art using their own developmentally appropriate language. Asking children intriguing questions will encourage them to tap their own intimate responses to art. Graphic organizers such as the Venn diagram and contrast frame will allow them to competently discuss the relative features of two dissimilar works of art, while a simple poetic structure can enable children to see that their own unique reactions to art constitute original poetry. Such poetry often becomes the final step in convincing children that their own responses to art really do have merit.

QUESTIONS FOR JOURNAL WRITING AND DISCUSSION

1. Reflect upon your first visit to an art gallery. What are your memories? What were your feelings about the paintings (drawings, sculptures, etc.) you saw? How were you able to respond to them? Did the visit make you feel more or less positive toward fine art? Why?
2. What do you think causes people to prefer one piece of artwrok over another? Do you think the preferences of adults are more valid than those of children? Why or why not? How much of an impact do you think exposure to art has on one's preferences?
3. Compose a rationale for introducing children to the creative works of artists from diverse cultures and artists who are women or people of color. How can such exposure help children to become more open to diversity?

SUGGESTIONS FOR PROJECTS

1. Select a reproduction of a fine art painting from an art appreciation text. Respond to the questions outlined in "Responding to the Paintings" in this chapter. Ask a friend or student in the class to answer the same questions pertaining to the same painting. Discuss the painting together using your responses as a starting point. How did your initial reflection and later discussion add to your enjoyment of the painting?

2. Read the biography of a famous artist, such as Mary Cassatt, Marc Chagall, or Pablo Picasso. Briefly share your findings about the life of the artist with the rest of the class. After "getting to know" the artist through the biography, has your appreciation and openness to the artist's works grown? To what extent? What implications does this have for classroom practice?

3. Take an intermediate-age child with you to a local art gallery. Record any comments the child makes about the artwork with no prompting. Then use the questions outlined in "Responding to the Paintings" in this chapter to induce reactions to the paintings. How do the questions change the quality and quantity of responses?

REFERENCES

Cain, M. (1989). *Mary Cassatt*. New York: Chelsea House.

Cudd, E. (1990). The paragraph frame: A bridge from narrative to expository text. In N. L. Cecil (Ed.), *Literacy in the 90's: Readings in the language arts* (pp. 172–182). Dubuque, IA: Kendall/Hunt Publishing Company.

Dobbs, S. M. (1988). Introduction. In S. M. Dobbs (Ed.), *Research reading for discipline-based art education: A journey beyond* (pp. 5–11). Reston, VA: National Art Education Association.

Eisner, E. (1987). The role of discipline-based art education in America's schools. *Art Education, 40,* 6–26, 43–45.

Godfrey, R. (1992). Civilization, education, and the visual arts: A personal manifesto. *Phi Delta Kappan, 73,* 596–600.

Lemay, P. (1990). Rudolf Nureyev. *Dance Magazine, 64,* 35–36.

Warner, S. (1989). *Encouraging the artist in your child even if you can't draw*. New York: St. Martin's Press.

CHAPTER 12

Classical Music: Wings for the Soul

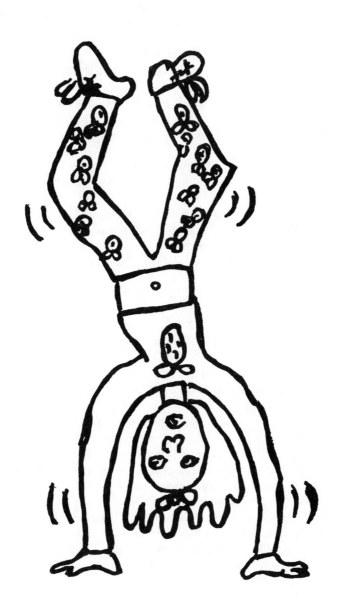

It is quite possible that, as the saying goes, children learn what they live.

One of the authors had the good fortune to grow up in a household continuously pervaded by classical music. She reminisces that her mother had once been a concert pianist and her earliest memories were of the strains of Beethoven's "Appassionata" coming from the baby grand piano in the living room. Moreover, the family was one of the last to give way to the ubiquitous television and, instead, Tchaikovsky or Schumann would fill the air from the stereo. The author doesn't actually remember responding to this music on a conscious level as a small child, but she does recall that by the time she became a teenager, she would sometimes (but not always) choose Rimsky-Korsakov to listen to over the then-popular Elton John. Classical music seemed to be edifying in a way that rock-and-roll—or currently, rap—could never be. Her soul would soar with the *The Nutcracker Suite*, or she could be soothed and sedated by the even cadence of Bach.

More recently, the relationship between musical ability and interest has become a puzzle to researchers (Hoffer, 1990) and the author: she played the flute in the high school band and then decided upon a career in music (which she later abandoned in favor of a teaching career). Had the interest, nurtured by continuous exposure to classical music, led to musical ability, or had some innate talent led to the interest?

Howard Gardner's theory of multiple intelligences (1983) has given rise to the notion that musical ability is a discrete intelligence, but that it can be fostered, to a degree, in *all* children by frequent exposure and by direct training. While the author does not suggest that teachers begin to believe that they can turn their entire class of children into budding Beethovens, it does now appear that some early association with quality music can not only increase all children's enjoyment of that art form, but also open windows of opportunity for those children who may already possess a modicum of musical talent.

A RATIONALE FOR INTEGRATING
CLASSICAL MUSIC AND LITERACY

Besides merely increasing children's aesthetic awareness and enjoyment, Christine Pappas, Barbara Kiefer, and Linda Levstik (1990) suggest that a sensitivity to the sounds of music can transfer to a greater appreciation of elements of sound in the outside world and its effect on human emotion conveyed through language. These authors feel that exposure to music can help children pay closer attention to the subtle qualities of pitch and volume in everyday auditory input as varied as an episode of the evening news, a speech, or a gospel preacher's sermon. Moreover, this fine-tuned awareness of the way language and other elements of the world's sounds might lead children to a heightened consciousness of their classroom and community environment, as well as to their own oral and written work.

To integrate music with literacy, however, the key word is *natural*. As naturally as children begin to babble and string words together into sentences, they can also begin to appreciate classical music as part of their world and be invited to offer their own personal reactions to it. One of the author's own memories, shared at the beginning of this chapter, was of a somewhat out-of-the-ordinary home life, where the family members were, on a daily basis, steeped in classical music. Can the same atmosphere "naturally" be infused into the elementary classroom? The remainder of this chapter will explore some answers to this question.

IDEAS FOR CLASSROOM PRACTICE

An integrated music and literacy program may begin even as early as kindergarten. Jeanenne Nichols, a kindergarten teacher in Abilene, Texas, systematically introduces and exposes children to quality music over the nine months of the school year (Nichols, 1991). Her model program can be adapted and enhanced to fit the needs of any elementary classroom.

Following are the selections Nichols has chosen for each month of the school year:

September: Vangelis. *Chariots of Fire.* Original soundtrack
Williams, John. *Star Wars.* Original soundtrack.

October: Dukas, Paul. *The Sorcerer's Apprentice.*
Saint-Saëns, Camille. *Danse Macabre.*
Debussy, Claude. *Prelude to the Afternoon of a Faun.*

November: Beethoven, Ludwig van. *Symphony no. 3 in F-flat Minor.* ("Eroica").
Bach, Johann Sebastian. *Toccata and Fugue in D Minor.*

December: Tchaikovsky, Peter Ilich. *The Nutcracker Suite.*
Handel, George Frideric. "Hallelujah Chorus," *Messiah.*

January: Prokofiev, Sergey Sergeyvich. *Peter and the Wolf.*
Telemann, Georg Philipp. *Concerto for Trumpet, String Orchestra, and Continuo in D Major.*
Telemann, Georg Philipp. *Concerto for Flute, String Orchestra, and Continuo in D Major.*
Telemann, Georg Philipp. *Concerto for Oboe, String Orchestra, and Continuo in E Major.*
Telemann, Georg Philipp. *Concerto for Viola, String Orchestra, and Continuo in G Major.*

February: Sousa, John Philip. *King Cotton.*
Sousa, John Philip. *Washington Post.*
Sousa, John Philip. *El Capitan.*
Sousa, John Philip. *The Thunderer.*
Sousa, John Philip. *The Stars and Stripes Forever.*

March: Copland, Aaron. *Billy the Kid.*
Handel, George Frideric. *Water Suite Music.*

April: Copland, Aaron. *Appalachian Spring Suite.*
Strauss, Johann. *Voices of Spring.*

May: Mozart, Wolfgang Amadeus. *Eine Kleine Nachtmusik.*
                    Bizet, Georges. "The Toreadors," *Carmen.*
                    Brahms, Johannes. *Symphony No. 1 in C Minor, Op. 18.*

Besides their initial introductions, these monthly selections are played when the children first come to class in the mornings, all during the opening exercises, and for a brief rest time after physical education.

The music has been selected, in some cases, for its theme. For example, *The Nutcracker Suite* and Handel's *Messiah* are both traditional holiday music, while *The Sorcerer's Apprentice* and *Danse Macabre* are each wonderful mood-setters for Halloween. Similarly, *Appalachian Spring Suite* and *Voices of Spring* were composed to suggest springtime images. Child-centered discussions center around how—or if—the composers accomplished their goals.

Other selections were grouped for different reasons. In January, the instruments of the orchestra are introduced through Prokofiev's *Peter and the Wolf*, where each animal is represented by a different instrument. The uniqueness of each instrument is reinforced through four Telemann concertos, each of which features a different instrument. February is John Philip Sousa month and children march to the rhythm of this brisk music for the entire 20 school days.

As each new piece of music is introduced to the children, Nichols uses a large beach ball globe to show where each composer was born. Children are encouraged to hypothesize how they would get from Abilene, Texas, to the birthplace of the various composers. Children also discuss how they think the people of a particular country, such as Prokofiev's Russia, talk, what they eat, and what their weather is like with the help of pictures from an encyclopedia and the teacher's input. Children soon reach an understanding that children in other countries laugh, play, go to school, and love their parents, siblings, and pets just as American children do.

Nichols also helps the children to brainstorm some ways that authors and composers are the same and different. Composers, for example, use notes to express their ideas and reach the hearts of listeners. By contrast, authors use words to create a story that may reach the hearts of its readers. On the other hand, as one youngster pointed out to her teacher, a story can "tell you things you didn't know before," or impart information, whereas a symphony probably cannot, at least in a factual sense.

To introduce the instruments in the orchestra, Nichols exposes children to three different versions of *Peter and the Wolf*. First, the stories are read without the music. Even kindergartners are able to discern the differing interpretations of the stories. Then the narrated recording of *Peter and the Wolf* is played. As the different animals and their corresponding instruments are introduced, Nichols uses a large poster of that instrument to make a visual impression, and all the children pretend to be playing the instrument as she demonstrates roughly how it would be played. The various instruments are reinforced, and new information about an orchestra, such as what the conductor does, is presented through an amusing book titled *Orchestranimals* (van Kampen & Eugen, 1989).

Older children may be ready to pick out the distinctive sounds of each of the instruments and begin to see how composers utilize different combinations of instruments to achieve various sound effects. To meet this objective, Nichols writes the names of several instruments on the chalkboard. Children express what each of the instruments reminds them of. For example, what images and emotions does a piccolo conjure up? How does a tuba make one feel? After a list has been developed for each of the instruments, children share why they think composers use certain instruments for one effect and not another.

Finally, children shut their eyes and listen to a piece of music that has already been heard before, but this time they listen for a specific instrument. After listening they tell how they recognize the instrument. Why do they feel the composer selected that instrument? Did they recognize the instrument by the images called up by its particular sounds, or did the sound-words that they brainstormed to describe it help them to identify it (Tiedt & Tiedt, 1989)?

Even mathematics can be brought into the music and literacy program as children are asked to respond to questions such as "Which instruments did you like best?" "Which instruments would you like most to play?" Or "Which character in *Peter and the Wolf* did you like the best?" Children then count the number of responses for each question, and the children, or the teacher for younger children, graph results.

MUSIC RESPONSE JOURNALS

Probably no group of people has a greater influence on today's children than do contemporary musicians, singers, and rap artists who seem to be affecting attitudes, fashions, and current vernacular along with musical trends. With older children, it is possible to develop a deeper appreciation of classical music by inviting them to respond in written form to music they already know and love. Ask children to bring in their favorite songs, and set aside a few minutes each day for the class to listen very carefully to each song. If possible, the lyrics should be written on a handout or on the overhead so that children may follow along.

As children listen to the first song, ask them to pay very close attention to the music as if they have never heard it before. Ask them to listen closely to the words, the instruments that have been chosen, the rhythms, and the mood that the music conveys. As they listen, invite them to quickly jot down any images, feelings, thoughts, colors, impressions, or comments that come to their minds. Explain that these images can be written in words or open-ended phrases. The resultant stream of consciousness is often remarkable as children have been encouraged to revisit familiar music with increased concentration and intensity.

Following is an excerpt from a music response journal written by one fifth-grade boy who had just listened intently to a contemporary song:

> I can see a bunch of soldiers marching up a high hill and then the enemy spies them and starts running after them . . . flashy green and black lights circling again and again. . . . You can tell they are winning now. . . . This part puts me in a mood where I would be winning the [basketball] game this afternoon because I could be all quick and really like powerful. . . . The good guys won the battle. . . . Now the soldiers are resting lying on the grass in front of their camps.

Because the teacher has attended to the students' music with respect, children are now open to listening more carefully to unfamiliar music. Subsequently, the teacher will want to select classical music with much dramatic intensity, such as Grieg's *Hall of the Mountain King* or Stravinsky's *Rites of Spring* or Rimsky-Korsakov's *Flight of the Bumblebee*. Invite them to get comfortable; ask them to relax, stretch out, and close their eyes. Tell them, "Imagine that your body has thousands and thousands of tiny pinpricks in it, so small that you can't even see them. Listen to the music and imagine that it must go through all those pinpricks before it can get inside of you. Once it gets through, it flows into all parts of you and fills you" (Chenfield, 1987). While children are in this mode, play the selected music for them. Afterward, encourage them to share their auditory images—the feelings, colors, words, and open-ended phrases they "saw"—just as they did with the more contemporary music. Finally, allow children to compare their responses in small share groups.

OTHER WAYS TO INTEGRATE MUSIC AND LITERACY

The children in Jeanenne Nichol's kindergarten also keep dialogue journals to respond to what the music says to them in their own personal ways. For most of the year, this communication consists of pictures portraying ideas and feelings that are then dictated to the teacher who transcribes them next to the child's picture. Toward the end of the year, some children can simply write their reactions to the music, adding illustrations if desired. The teacher then reads the children's entries, comments on their ideas, and asks questions to keep the dialogue going.

For older children, poetry is a natural way to express their reactions to classical music. As children become able to think more abstractly, they are then able to articulate what poetry and music have in common. When children have had some experience with both art forms, for example, they can be drawn into a discussion as to how Strauss's *Voices of Spring* evokes similar or different images from e. e. cummings's *in just spring*.

Debussy's *La Mer* is a piece of music that is called a "tone poem" because of the dreamlike way it musically describes the sea and the emotions associated with it. Using this or a similar piece of music, teachers can encourage children to brainstorm the images that the music brings forth from them. The children can then use these images in free verse to write their own poetic reaction to the music. A haiku is suitable for older children, while the five senses format (see chapter 8) is better for younger children.

After children have finished writing their poems, they can be encouraged to tell how their own writing made them feel about the music: Do they now feel "closer" to the music? Do some children respond differently than others? Why? Children will begin to understand how capturing the essence of the piece through poetry may help them to internalize and better appreciate the music.

With yet another listening to the same piece of music, children may be invited to share any new facets of the piece that they had not noticed before. Music can be a fresh, new experience each time it is heard. Finally, children can be encouraged to read their poems aloud to the rest of the class while the music is playing in the background. Children will naturally discover through this simultaneous event that "the music is illustrating the poem and the poem is illustrating the music" (Tiedt & Tiedt, 1989).

Children in the upper grades can also begin to write their reactions to music in a different way, using the vehicle of the contrast frame (Cudd, 1990). This device provides a literacy scaffold, or temporary structure for the children to use so that they may begin to record their observations in an expository mode. While such a device is useful in helping all children to organize their ideas, it is especially helpful for children for whom English is a second language as they begin to acquire literacy skills.

To use a contrast frame, two pieces of classical music are selected that are very different from one another, such as Grieg's *Morning* and *Hall of the Mountain King*; or Handel's *Pastorale* and Mendelssohn's *The Hebrides Overture*. After listening to each piece separately, children brainstorm descriptive words or phrases that tell how each piece makes them feel, or what it reminds them of. Children may offer words, phrases, or any bits of descriptive imagery. After they have brainstormed with both pieces of music, the following contrast frame can be used as a way for children to summarize what they feel are the differences between the two pieces of music:

Contrast Frame
"The Hall of the Mountain King" and "Morning" differ in several ways. First, "The Hall of the Mountain King" is _____, while "Morning" is _____. Second, "The Hall of the Mountain King" is _____, while "Morning" is _____. Probably the way the two pieces of music are most different is _____.

As a more personal alternative, children may enjoy sharing orally, or in written form, their responses to the following questions regarding the two pieces of music: "Which of these two pieces best expresses how you are feeling today?" "What aspect of the piece is like your mood today (the instruments, the pace, etc.)?" Children may also wish to illustrate their ideas.

Pappas, Kiefer, and Levstik (1990) offer several other suggestions for integrating music with literacy in the elementary school:

- Discuss the variety of musical forms in your culture.
- Compare music in your culture with that of other cultures.
- Make your own musical instruments.
- Choose classical music as a theme for a story or novel.
- Orchestrate a poem for choral reading.
- Listen to sounds in the city or in nature; represent the pitches on a musical scale, using a xylophone or glasses of water at varying levels.

THE QUESTION OF MUSICAL BACKGROUND

As with any of the arts, teachers' backgrounds will vary widely, yet teachers need not feel that they require an extensive understanding of musical forms or familiarity with all of the most well-known composers in order to competently integrate music with literacy. As with other arts, the process of responding to classical music is more critical than any products that may result; an enthusiasm for and an appreciation of classical music is the foremost concern. Moreover, learning right along with the children is often a very pleasant change of pace for teachers and a welcome anxiety-reducer for children who too often perceive their teachers as knowing everything about everything.

The most powerful learning takes place as teachers ask children—and children ask teachers and each other—questions that help them develop their own aesthetic awareness and their own linguistic power to discuss that awareness. "What were you thinking about as you listened to that music?" Or "How did that symphony make you feel? What makes you feel that way?" These are questions that any sensitive teacher can ask.

If, however, teachers have some background in classical music, they may want to share their knowledge of some of the terminology associated with different forms of music. Just as the language arts teacher uses the terms *character, setting, plot, story,* and so forth to discuss writing, teachers may feel free to use terms such as *largo, allegro,* and *staccato,* if they are familiar with them, to help children understand how musicians think and talk about their art form. This specialized language then empowers children to talk in what they will consider to be a "sophisticated" way about their own aesthetic responses to music (Gardner & Winner, 1982).

SUMMARY

Classical music can make the spirit soar, but all children may not have been exposed to this artistic medium in their homes. However, continuous exposure to selected musical compositions, as addressed in this chapter, can foster an appreciation for classical music in most students and perhaps awaken nascent musical ability in others.

By utilizing a wide variety of language activities, such as journal writing, discussion, brainstorming, poetry writing, and the use of contrast frames, children can begin to express their thoughts and feelings about what they are hearing. Moreover, through an introduction to the instruments of the orchestra, their discrete sounds, and how they are combined to evoke images, children will begin to see music as another communication system particularly suited to express emotions.

Most importantly, the integration of music and literacy can unite hearts and minds in a unique way. With today's classrooms becoming more and more heterogeneous gardens of children who speak many different languages, it is the hope of the authors of this text that music will soon be considered essential in the elementary curriculum. It is, after all, the "universal language."

QUESTIONS FOR JOURNAL WRITING AND DISCUSSION

1. What is your favorite kind of music? Describe why you like it and how it makes you feel. How much exposure have you received to this kind of music? How much connection do you feel there is between exposure to a particular kind of music and enjoyment of that music?
2. Make a list of all the music in your environment in a typical day, such as listening to the car radio on the way to work, background music in the supermarket, and so on. Describe how you think music enriches your life.
3. Explain what you think is meant by the statement "Music is a universal language." Do all people hear the same things when they listen to a piece of music? How can personal responses to music be conveyed to those who speak no English? Why is music an important component for a multicultural classroom?

SUGGESTIONS FOR PROJECTS

1. Obtain a copy of one of the classical music selections mentioned in this chapter. Over a period of several days, play the piece often as background music while you are doing household chores; at a later time, listen to the music intently using the auditory imaging procedure explained in this chapter. Afterward, jot down words, impressions, thoughts, and open-ended phrases that describe how the music made you feel. On a later, separate occasion, listen to the music once more. Has your appreciation for the piece of music grown? Would the same procedure be effective with young children?
2. Survey a group of children of similar ages. Ask them to tell you what kind of music they listen to and to describe why they like it. Ask them also to tell you what kind of music they do *not* like and to describe why they do *not* like it. On the basis of children's responses, describe what you think might be an appropriate path for a teacher to take in the classroom to lead students from an enjoyment of contemporary music toward an appreciation of classical music.
3. Interview a music teacher in your district. Ask him or her if and when children are exposed to classical music in the K–6 music curriculum. How often? How are they helped to appreciate classical music? Are they given any opportunity to orally share their responses to music? Share your findings with the members of your class.

REFERENCES

Chenfield, M. B. (1987). *Teaching language arts creatively* (2nd ed.). San Diego: Harcourt Brace Jovanovich.

Cudd, E. (1990). The paragraph frame: A bridge from narrative to expository text. In N. L. Cecil (Ed.), *Literacy in the 90's*. Dubuque, IA: Kendall/Hunt.

Gardner, H. (1983). *Frames of mind: The theory of multiple intelligences*. New York: Basic Books.

Gardner, H., & Winner, E. (1982). Children's conceptions (and misconceptions) of the arts. In H. Gardner, *Art, mind, and brain: A cognitive approach to creativity* (pp. 103–109). New York: Basic Books.

Hoffer, C. (1990). Artistic intelligence and music education. In W. J. Moody (Ed.), *Artistic intelligence: Implications for education* (pp. 135–140). New York: Teachers College Press.

Nichols, J. (1991). Music notes on a kindergarten scale: Integrating classical music with content area. *Reading Excellence Through the Arts Newsletter.*

Pappas, C., Kiefer, B., & Levstik, L. (1990). *An integrated language perspective in the elementary school: Theory into action.* New York: Longman.

Tiedt, S., & Tiedt, I. (1989). *Language arts activities for the classroom.* Boston: Allyn & Bacon.

van Kampen, V., & Eugen, I. (1989) *Orchestranimals.* New York: Scholastic.

A Bibliography of Children's Literature about the Arts

The following list is divided into six main sections—Art, Dance, Drama, Music, Photography, and Poetry. Within each section are categories listing, for example, Expressive Art, Art as Theme, and Art History and Art Appreciation. References are coded "P" for preschool and early primary readers, "I" for books suitable for intermediate readers, and "MC" for books with a multicultural component.

ART

Expressive Art

Adkins, J. (1975). *Inside: Seeing beneath the surface.* New York: Walker. (I)

Albenda, P. (1970). *Creative painting with tempera.* New York: Van Nostrand.

Aliki. (1986). *How a book is made.* New York: Harper & Row. (P)

Arnosky, J. (1982). *Drawing from nature.* New York: Lothrop. (P, I)

Blegvad, E. (1979). *Self-portrait: Eric Blegvad.* Reading, MA: Addison Wesley. (I, MC)

Bolognese, D., & Thornton, R. (1983). *Drawing and painting with the computer.* New York: Franklin Watts. (P, I)

Emberley, E. (1991). *Ed Emberley's drawing book: Make a world.* Boston: Little, Brown. (P)

Evans, J., & Moore, J. E. (1985). *How to make books with children.* Monterey, CA: Evan Moore. (P)

Fischer, L. E. (1986). *The papermakers.* Boston: David Godine. (P)

Galate, L. (1980). *A beginner's guide to calligraphy.* New York: Dell. (I)

Graham, A., & Stoke, D. (1983). *Fossils, ferns, and fish scales: A handbook of art and nature projects.* New York: Four Winds. (I)

Hyman, T. S. (1981). *Self-portrait: Trina Schart Hyman.* Reading, MA: Addison Wesley. (I)

Irvine, J., & Reid, B. (1987). *How to make pop-ups.* New York: William Morrow. (P, I)

Joe, E. (1978). *Navajo sandpainting art.* Tucson, AZ: Treasure Chest. (I, MC)

Kohl, M. (1989). *Mudworks*. Bellingham, WA: Bright Ring. (P, I)

Kohl, M., & Gainer, C. (1991). *Good earth art: Environmental art for kids*. Bellingham, WA: Bright Ring. (P, I)

Marks, M. (1972). *OP-tricks: Creating kinetic art*. Philadelphia: J. B. Lippincott. (I)

Muller, B. (1987). *Painting with children*. Edinburgh, Scotland: Floris Books. (P, I)

Pluckrose, H. (1989). *Crayons*. New York: Watts. (P)

Reid, B. (1989). *Playing with plasticine*. Long Beach, CA: Beechtree Books. (P, I)

Sakata, H. (1990). *Origami*. New York: Japan Publishers, U.S.A. (I, MC)

Solga, K. (1992). *Make sculptures*. Cincinnati: North Light Books. (P, I)

Stangl, J. (1986). *Magic mixtures*. Carthage, IL: Teaching Aids. (P, I)

Takahama, T. (1988). *Quick and easy origami*. New York: Japan Publications. (I, MC)

Webb, P. H., & Corby, J. (1991). *Shadowgraphs anyone can make*. New York: Running Press. (I)

Weiss, H. (1988). *Pencil, pen, and brush: Drawing for beginners*. New York: Scholastic. (P, I)

Weiss, P., & Giralla, S. (1976). *Simple printmaking*. New York: Lothrop. (P, I)

Zemach, M. (1978). *Self-portrait: Margot Zemach*. Reading, MA: Addison Wesley. (I)

Art as Theme

Abby Aldrich Rockefeller Folk Art Center (1991). *The folk art counting book*. New York: Abrams. (P)

Agee, J. (1988). *The incredible painting of Felix Clousseau*. New York: Farrar, Straus, & Giroux. (I)

Blood, C., & Link, M. (1990). *The goat in the rug*. New York: Aladdin-Macmillan Child Group. (P, MC)

Byars, B. (1978). *The cartoonist*. New York: Viking. (I)

Canning, K. (1979). *A painted tale*. New York: Barron's. (P)

Carrick, D. (1985). *Morgan and the artist*. New York: Clarion. (P)

Clement, C. (1986). *The painter and the wild swans*. New York: Pied Piper–Dial. (P, MC)

Coerr, E. (1986). *The Josefina story quilt*. New York: Harper Trophy. (P)

Cohen, M., & Hoban, L. (1980). *No good in art*. New York: Greenwillow. (P)

Craven, C., & dePaola, T. (1989). *What the mailman brought*. New York: G. P. Putnam's Sons. (P)

Demi, L. (1988). *Liang and the magic paintbrush*. New York: Henry Holt. (P, MC).

dePaola, T. (1989). *The art lesson*. New York: Putnam. (P)

dePaola, T. (1988). *The legend of the Indian paintbrush*. New York: G. P. Putnam's Sons. (P, MC)

de Trevino, E. B. (1965). *I, Juan de Pareja*. New York: Farrar, Straus, & Giroux. (I, MC)

Ernst, L. C. (1986). *Hamilton's art show*. New York: Lothrop. (P)

French, F. (1977). *Matteo*. New York: Oxford University Press. (P, I)

Grifalconi, A. (1990). *Osa's pride*. Boston: Little, Brown. (P, MC)

Heyer, M. (1986). *The weaving of a dream*. New York: Puffin. (I, MC)

Isadora, R. (1988). *The pirates of Bedford Street*. New York: Greenwillow. (P)

Kesselman, W., & Cooney, B. (1980). *Emma*. New York: Doubleday. (P)

Konigsburg, E. L. (1967). *From the mixed-up files of Mrs. Basil E. Frankweiler*. New York: Atheneum. (I)

Leaf, M. (1987). *Eyes of the dragon*. New York: Lothrop, Lee, & Shephard. (I, MC)

Lobel, A. (1968). *The great blueness and other predicaments*. New York: Harper & Row. (P)

Locker, T. (1989). *The young artist*. New York: Dial. (I)

Mayers, F. (1991). *The ABC: Museum of Fine Arts, Boston*. New York: Abrams. (P)

Mayers, F. (1991). *The ABC: Museum of Modern Art, New York*. New York: Abrams. (P)
McPhail, D. (1978). *The magical drawings of Mooney B. Finch*. New York: Doubleday. (P)
O'Kelley, M. L. (1983). *From the hills of Georgia: An autobiography in paintings*. Boston: Atlantic Monthly. (I)
Paterson, K. (1979). *Bridge to Terabithia*. New York: Harper & Row. (I)
Picard, B. L. (1966). *One is one*. New York: Henry Holt. (I)
Polacco, P. (1988). *The keeping quilt*. New York: Simon & Schuster. (I)
Rylant, C., & Catalanotto, P. (1988). *All I see*. New York: Orchard. (I)
Sanford, J. (1991). *Slappy Hooper: The world's greatest sign painter*. New York: Warner. (P)
Schick, E. (1987). *Art lessons*. New York: Greenwillow. (P)
Small, D. (1987). *Paper John*. New York: Farrar, Straus, & Giroux. (P)
Spier, P. (1978). *Oh, were they ever happy!* New York: Doubleday. (P)
Stecher, M. (1980). *Max the music maker*. New York: Lothrop. (P)
Sutcliff, R. (1978). *Sun horse, moon horse*. New York: Dutton. (P)
Tuyet, Tran-Khan. (1987). *The little weaver of Thai-Yen village*. Emeryville, CA: Children's Book Press. (P, MC)
Wadell, M., & Langley, J. (1988). *Alice the artist*. New York: Dutton. (P, I)
Walsh, E. S. (1990). *Mouse paint*. Niles, IL: Harcourt, Brace, Jovanovich. (P)
Xiong, B. (1989). *Nine-in-one, grr, grr*. Emeryville, CA: Children's Book Press. (P, MC)

Art History and Appreciation

Behrens, J. (1977). *Looking at beasties*. Chicago: Children's Press. (P)
Behrens, J. (1982). *Looking at children*. Chicago: Children's Press. (P, I)
Bjork, C., & Anderson, L. (1985). *Linnea in Monet's garden*. New York: R & S Books. (P, I)
Blizzard, G. (1992). *Come look with me: Exploring landscape art with children*. Charlottsville, VA: Thomasson-Grant. (P, I)
Bohn-Ducher, M., & Cook, J. (1991). *Understanding modern art*. London: Osborn House. (I)
Bonafoux, P. (1987). *van Gogh: The passionate eye*. New York: Abrams. (I)
Bonafoux, P. (1991). *A weekend with Rembrandt*. New York: Rizzoli International. (I)
Brown, L. K., & Brown, M. (1986). *Visiting the art museum*. New York: Dutton. (P, I)
Cachin, F. (1991). *Gauguin: The quest for paradise*. New York: Abrams. (I)
Ceserani, G. P., & Ventura, P. (1983). *Grand constructions*. New York: G. P. Putnam's Sons. (I)
Conner, P. (1982). *Looking at art: People at home*. New York: Atheneum. (P, I)
Conner, P. (1982). *Looking at art: People at work*. New York: Atheneum. (P, I)
Craft, R. (1975). *Brueghal's the fair*. New York: J. B. Lippincott. (I)
Cummings, P. (1992). *Talking with artists*. New York: Bradbury. (P, I)
Cummings, R. (1979). *Just look: A book about paintings*. New York: Scribner. (P, I)
Cummings, R. (1982). *Just imagine: Ideas in painting*. New York: Scribner. (P, I)
Davidson, M. B. (1984). *A history of art*. New York: Random House. (P)
Drucker, M. (1991). Frida Kahlo: *Torment and triumph in her life and art*. New York: Bantam. (I, MC)
Fine, J., & Anderson, D. (1979). *I carve stone*. New York: Crowell. (P)
Gates, F. (1982). *North American Indian masks: Craft and legend*. New York: Walker. (I, MC)
Gherman, B. (1986). *Georgia O'Keeffe*. New York: Atheneum. (I)
Glubok, S., & Nook, G. (1972). *The art of the new American*. New York: Macmillan. (I)
Goffstein, M. B. (1983). *Lives of the artists*. New York: Harper & Row. (I)
Greenfeld, H. (1991). *Marc Chagall*. New York: Abrams. (I)

Highwater, J. (1978). *Many smokes, many moons: A chronology of American Indian history through Indian art*. New York: J. B. Lippincott. (I, MC)

Holmes, B. (1979). *Enchanted worlds: Pictures to grow up with*. New York: Universal Press. (P, I)

Holmes, B. (1980). *Creatures of paradise: Pictures to grow up with*. New York: University Press. (P, I)

Janson, H. W., & Janson, A. F. (1992). *History of art for young people*. New York: Abrams. (I)

Kennet, F., & Measham, T. (1979). *Looking at paintings*. New York: Van Nostrand Reinhold. (P, I)

Klein, M., & Klein, H. (1972). *Kathe Kollwitz: Life in art*. New York: Holt, Rinehart, & Winston. (I)

Lepscky, I. (1984). *Pablo Picasso*. Woodbury, NY: Barron's. (I)

Macauley, D. (1973). *Cathedral: The story of its construction*. Boston: Houghton Mifflin. (I)

McLanathan, R. (1991). *Leonardo da Vinci*. New York: Abrams. (I)

Meyer, S. (1990). *Mary Cassatt*. New York: Abrams. (I)

Munthe, N., & Kee, R. (1983). *Meet Matisse*. Boston: Little, Brown. (I)

Nelson, M. (1972). *Maria Martinez*. New York: Dodd Mead. (I, MC)

Newlands, A., & National Gallery of Canada staff (1989). *Meet Edgar Degas*. New York: Harper Child Books. (P, I)

Oneal, Z. (1986). *Grandma Moses: Painter of rural America*. New York: Viking/Kestrel. (I)

Price, C. (1977). *Arts of clay*. New York: Scribner. (I)

Priess, B. (1981). *The art of Leo and Diane Dillon*. New York: Ballantine. (I)

Proddow, P. (1979). *Art tells a story: Greek and Roman myths*. New York: Doubleday. (P, I)

Provenson, A., & Provenson, M. (1984). *Leonardo da Vinci*. New York: Viking. (I)

Raboff, E. (1982). *Marc Chagall*. Garden City, NY: Doubleday. (I)

Raboff, E. (1982). *Paul Klee*. Garden City, NY: Doubleday. (I)

Raboff, E. (1982) *Pablo Picasso*. Garden City, NY: Doubleday. (I)

Raboff, E. Art for Children series. *da Vinci* (1987); *Rembrandt* (1987); *Renoir* (1987); *Henri Matisse* (1988); *Michelangelo* (1988); *Raphael* (1988); *Velasquez* (1988); *Vincent van Gogh* (1988). New York: J. B. Lippincott. (I)

Roalf, P. Looking at Painting series: *Dancers* (1992); *Cats* (1992); *Families* (1992); *Seascapes* (1992). New York: Hyperion. (P, I)

Rockwell, A. (1971). *Paintbrush and peace pipe: The story of George Catlin*. New York: Atheneum. (I, MC)

Rodari, F. (1990). *A weekend with Picasso*. New York: Rizzoli International. (I)

Schwartz, L. (1992). *Rembrandt*. New York: Abrams. (I)

Sills, L. (1989). *Inspirations: Stories about women artists*. Nills, IL: Whitman. (I)

Skira-Venturi, R. (1990). *A weekend with Renoir*. New York: Rizzoli International. (I)

Tobias, T. (1974). *Isamu Noguchi: The life of a sculptor*. New York: Crowell. (I, MC)

Turner, R. (1991). *Georgia O'Keeffe*. Boston: Little, Brown. (I)

Venezia, M. Getting to Know the World's Great Artists series. *Picasso* (1988); *Rembrandt* (1988): *van Gogh* (1988); *da Vinci* (1989); *Mary Cassatt* (1990); *Edward Hopper* (1990); *Monet* (1990); *Botticelli* (1991); *Goya* (1991); *Paul Klee* (1991); *Michelangelo* (1991). Chicago: Children's Press. (I)

Ventura, P. (1984). *Great painters*. New York: Putnam. (I)

Ventura, P. (1989). *Michelangelo's world*. New York: G. P. Putnam's Sons. (I)

Walters, A. (1989). *The spirit of native America: Beauty and mysticism in American Indian art*. San Francisco: Chronicle. (I, MC)

Waterfield, G. (1982). *Looking at art: Faces*. New York: Atheneum. (P, I)

Winter, J. (1991). *Diego*. New York: Alfred Knopf. (I, MC)

Woolf, F. (1989). *Picture this: A first introduction to paintings*. New York: Doubleday. (P)
Yenawine, P., & Museum of Modern Art. Series on Modern Art. *Colors* (1991); *Lines* (1991); *Shapes* (1991); *Stories* (1991). New York: Delacorte Press. (P, I)
Zhensun, Z., & Low, A. (1991). *A young painter: The life and paintings of Wang Yani, China's extraordinary artist*. New York: Scholastic. (I, MC)

DANCE

Dance as Theme

Ackerman, K., & Gammell, S. (1988). *Song and dance man*. New York: Alfred Knopf. (P)
dePaola, T. (1979). *Oliver Button is a sissy*. San Diego: Harcourt Brace Jovanovich. (P)
French, V. (1991). *One ballerina two*. New York: Lothrop. (P)
Gauch, P. (1989). *Bravo Tanya*. New York: G. P. Putnam's Sons. (P)
Getz, A. (1980). *Humphrey the dancing pig*. New York: Dial. (P)
Holabird, K. (1992). *Angelina dances*. New York: Random House Books for Young Readers. (P)
Hurd, E. (1982). *I dance in my red pajamas*. New York: Harper & Row. (P, I)
Kuklin, S. (1989). *Going to my ballet class*. New York: Macmillan. (P)
Martin, B., & Archambault, J., & Rand, T. (1986). *Barn dance*. New York: Henry Holt. (P, I)
Oxenbury, H. (1983). *The dancing class*. New York: Dial. (P)
Schroeder, A. (1989). *Ragtime Tumpie*. New York: Little, Brown. (I, MC)
Simon, C. (1989). *Amy, the dancing bear*. New York: Doubleday. (P)
Waters, K., & Slovenz-Low, M. (1990). *Lion dancer: Earnie Wan's Chinese New Year*. (I, MC)

Dance History and Appreciation

Anderson, H. C. (1991). *The Red Shoes*. New York: Simon & Schuster Children's Books. (I)
Dood, C., & Soar, S. (1988). *Ballet in motion: A three-dimensional guide to ballet for young people*. New York: J. B. Lippincott. (I)
Fonteyn, M. (1989). *Swan Lake*. San Diego: Gulliver. (I)
Haskins, J. (1990). *Black dance in America: A history through its people*. New York: Crowell. (I, MC)
Helprin, M. (1989). *Swan Lake*. Boston: Houghton Mifflin. (I)
Hoffman, E. T. (1984). *The Nutcracker*. New York: Crown. (P, I)
Verdy, V. (1991). *Of swans, sugarplums, and satin slippers: Ballet stories for children*. New York: Scholastic. (P, I)
Werner. V. (1992). *Petrouchka*. New York: Viking Children's Books. (I)

DRAMA

Expressive Drama

Carlson, B. W. (1982). *Let's find the big idea*. Nashville: Abingdon. (I)
Davis, O. (1978). *Escape to freedom: A play about Frederick Douglass*. New York: Viking. (I, MC)
Dunn, S. (1990). *Crackers and crumbs: Chants for whole language*. Portsmouth, NH: Heinemann. (I)

Jennings, C. A., & Harris, A. (1981). *Plays children love: A treasury of contemporary and classic plays for children*. Garden City, N.J.: Doubleday. (I)

Jennings, C. A. & Harris, A. (Eds.). (1988). *Plays children love*. Vol. 2. New York: St. Martin's Press. (I)

McDonald, M. R. (1986). *Twenty tellable tales: Audience participation folktales for the beginning storyteller*. New York: Wilson. (I)

Willard, N. (1989). *East of the sun and west of the moon: A play*. San Diego: Harcourt Brace Jovanovich. (I)

Winther, B. (1992). *Plays from African tales*. Boston: Plays, Inc. (I, MC)

Drama as Theme

Blume, J. (1981). *The one in the middle is a green kangaroo*. New York: Yearling. (P)

Brandenberg, F. (1977). *Nice new neighbors*. New York: Scholastic. (P)

Byers, B. (1992). *Hooray for the Golly sisters!* New York: Harper Children's Books. (I)

Cohen, M. (1985). *Starring first grade*. New York: Greenwillow. (P)

dePaola, T. (1978) *The Christmas pageant*. Houston, TX: Winston Press. (P, I)

dePaola, T. (1983). *Sing, Pierrot, sing: A picture book in mime*. New York: Harcourt Brace Jovanovich.

De Regniers, B. (1982). *Picture book theater: The mysterious stranger and the magic spell*. San Francisco: (Seabury Press) Harper & Row. (P)

Giff, P. (1984). *The almost awful play*. New York: Viking. (P)

Hoffman, M. (1991). *Amazing Grace*. New York: Dial Books. (P, I, MC)

Holabird, K. (1986). *Angelina on stage*. New York: Crown. (P)

Howard. E. (1991). *Aunt Flossie's hats (and crab cakes later)*. Boston: Houghton Mifflin. (P)

Marshall, E. (1981). *Three by the sea*. New York: Dial. (P)

Martin, A. M. (1984). *Stage fright*. New York: Holiday House. (I)

Oppenheim, J. (1984). *Mrs. Peloki's class play*. New York: Dodd Mead. (P)

Sendak, M. (1976). *Maurice Sendak's Really Rosie: Starring the nutshell kids*. New York: Harper & Row. (P)

MUSIC

Expressive Music

Aliki. (1968). *Hush, little baby*. New York: Prentice-Hall. (P)

Aliki. (1974). *Go tell Aunt Rhody*. New York: Macmillan. (P)

Axelrod, A. (1991). *Songs of the wild west*. Metropolitan Museum of Art. New York: Simon & Schuster. (I)

Bantok, N. (1990). *There was an old lady*. New York: Viking/Penguin. (P)

Barbareski, N. (1985). *Frog went a-courting*. New York: Scholastic. (P)

Bierhorst, J. (1979). *A cry from the earth: Music of the North American Indians*. New York: Four Winds. (I, MC)

Brett, J. (1990). *The twelve days of Christmas*. New York: G. P. Putnam's Sons. (P, I)

Bryan, A. (1991). *All night, all day: A child's first book of African-American spirituals*. New York: Atheneum. (P, MC)

Bunting, J. (1980). *My first recorder and book*. New York: Barron's. (P)

Child, L. (1987). *Over the river and through the woods*. New York: Scholastic. (P)

Cole, J., & Calmenson, S. (1991). *The eentsy, weentsy spider: Fingerplays and action rhymes.* New York: Mulberry Book. (P)

Cooney, B., & Griego, M. C. (1981). *Tortillitas para mama and other nursery rhymes.* Spanish/English. New York: Henry Holt. (P, MC)

Delacre, L. (1989). *Arroz con leche: Popular songs and rhymes from Latin America.* New York: Scholastic. (P, I, MC)

Disney Press (1991). *For our children.* Burbank: Disney Press. (P)

Durell, A. (1989). *The Diane Goode book of American folk tales and songs.* New York: Dutton Child Books. (P, I, MC)

Girl Scouts of U.S.A. (1980). *Canciones de nuestra cabana: Songs of our cabana.* New York: Girl Scouts of U.S.A. (P, I, MC)

Glass, P. (1969). *Singing soldiers: A history of the Civil War in song.* New York: Grosset & Dunlap. (P, I)

Glazer, T. (1980). *Do your ears hang low? Fifty more musical fingerplays.* New York: Doubleday. (P)

Glazer, T. (1982). *On top of spaghetti.* New York: Doubleday. (P)

Glazer, T. (1988). *Tom Glazer's treasury of songs for children.* New York: Doubleday. (P, I)

Glazer, T. (1990). *The Mother Goose songbook.* New York: Doubleday. (P)

Griego, F. M. (1980). *Tortillas para mama.* New York: Holt, Rinehart, & Winston. (P, I, MC)

Hart, J. (1992). *Singing bee! A collection of favorite children's songs.* New York: Lothrop, Lee, & Shephard. (P, I)

Hawkinson, J., & Faulhaber, M. (1969). *Music and instruments for children to make.* Niles, IL: Whitman. (P, I)

Houston, J. (1972). *Song of the dream people: Chants and images of the Indians and Eskimos of North America.* New York: Atheneum. (P, I, MC)

Keats, E. (1972). *Over in the meadow.* New York: Scholastic. (P)

Kellogg, S. (1976). *Yankee doodle.* New York: Parents' Magazine Press. (P)

Kennedy, J. (1983). *Teddy bear's picnic.* San Marcos, CA: Green Tiger Press. (P)

Knight, H. (1981). *The twelve days of Christmas.* New York: Macmillan. (P)

Koontz, R. (1988). *This old man: The counting song.* New York: G. P. Putnam's Sons. (P)

Kovalski, M. (1987). *The wheels on the bus.* Boston: Little, Brown. (P)

Krull, K. (1989). *Songs of praise.* San Diego: Harcourt Brace Jovanovich. (P, I)

Langstaff, J. (1974). *Oh, a-hunting we will go.* New York: Atheneum. (P)

Leedy, L. (1988). *The bunny play.* New York: Holiday House. (P)

Livingston, M. (1986). *Earth songs.* New York: Holiday House. (P, I)

Livingston, M. (1986). *Sea songs.* New York: Holiday House. (P, I)

Magers, P. (1987). *Sing with me animal songs.* New York: Random House. (P)

Mattox, C. (1990). *Shake it to the one that you love best: Play songs and lullabies from black musical tradition.* El Sobrante, CA: Warren Mattox. (I, MC)

McNally, D. (1991). *In a cabin in a wood.* New York: Cobblehill Dutton. (P)

Metropolitan Museum of Art staff (1987). *Go in and out the window: An illustrated songbook for young people.* New York: Henry Holt. (P, I)

National Gallery of Art. (1991). *An illustrated treasury of songs: Traditional American songs, ballads, folk songs, nursery rhymes.* New York: Rizzoli International. (P, I, MC)

Paterson, A. B. (1972). *Waltzing Matilda.* New York: Holt, Rinehart, & Winston. (P)

Pearson, T. C. (1985). *Sing a song of sixpence.* New York: Dial. (P)

Peek, M. (1981). *Roll over! A counting song.* Boston: Houghton Mifflin. (P)

Peek, M. (1987). *The balancing act: A counting song.* New York: Clarion. (P)

Peek, M. (1988). *Mary wore her red dress and Henry wore his green sneakers.* Boston: Houghton Mifflin. (P)

Quackenbush, T. C. (1973). *She'll be coming 'round the mountain*. New York: Dial. (P)

Quackenbush, T. C. (1975). *The man on the flying trapeze*. Philadelphia: J. B. Lippincott. (P)

Rae, M. M. (1989). *The farmer in the dell*. New York: Scholastic. (P)

Raffi. (1987). *Down by the bay*. New York: Crown. (P)

Raffi. (1989). *The Raffi everything grows songbook*. New York: Crown. (P)

Rounds, G. (1989). *Old MacDonald had a farm*. New York: Holiday House. (P)

Seeger, P. (1989). *Abiyoyo*. New York: Scholastic. (P, MC)

Spier, P. (1961). *The fox went out on a chilly night*. New York: Doubleday. (P)

Spier, P. (1967). *London bridge is falling down*. New York: Doubleday. (P)

Walther, T. (1981). *Make mine music*. Boston: Little, Brown. (I)

Wessells, K. (1982). *The golden songbook*. New York: Golden. (P)

Westcott, N. (1980). *I know an old lady who swallowed a fly*. Boston: Little, Brown. (P)

Westcott, N. (1989). *Skip to my Lou*. Boston: Little, Brown. (P)

Williams, V. (1988). *Music, music for everyone*. New York: Morrow. (P, I)

Winter, J. (1988). *Follow the drinking gourd*. New York: Alfred Knopf. (P)

Wiserman, A. (1979). *Making musical things*. New York: Scribner. (P, I)

Yokum, J. (1986). *The lullaby songbook*. San Diego: Harcourt Brace Jovanovich. (P)

Music as Theme

Ackerman, K., & Gammell, S. (1988). *Song and dance man*. New York: Alfred Knopf. (P)

Angell, J. (1982). *Buffalo nickel blues band*. New York: Bradbury. (I)

Bang, M. (1985). *The paper crane*. New York: Greenwillow. (P)

Baylor, B., & Himler, R. (1982). *Moon song*. New York: Scribner. (P)

Birdseye, T., & Gammell, S. (1988). *Airmail to the moon*. New York: Holiday House. (P)

Bodecker, N. M. (1981). *The lost string quartet*. New York: Atheneum. (P)

Boynton, S. (1979). *Hester in the wild*. New York: Harper & Row. (P)

Brett, J. (1991). *Berlioz the bear*. New York: G. P. Putnam's Sons. (P)

Buffett, J., & Buffett, S. J. (1988). *The jolly mon*. New York: Harcourt Brace Jovanovich. (P)

Bunting, E., & Zemach, K. (1983). *The traveling men of Ballycoo*. New York: Harcourt Brace Jovanovich. (P)

Burningham, J. (1984). *Granpa*. New York: Crown. (P)

Byars, B. (1985). *The glory girl*. New York: Puffin Books. (I)

Carlson, N. (1983). *Loudmouth George and the cornet*. Minneapolis: Carolrhoda. (P)

dePaola, T. (1979). *Oliver Button is a sissy*. New York: Harcourt Brace Jovanovich. (P)

Duder, T. (1986). *Jellybean*. New York: Viking. (I)

Dupasquier, P. (1985). *Dear Daddy*. New York: Bradbury. (P)

Edwards, P. K., & Allison, D. (1987). *Chester and Uncle Willoughby*. Boston: Little, Brown. (P)

Fleischman, P., & Wentworth, J. (1988). *Rondo in C*. New York: Harper & Row. (P)

Gilson, J. (1979). *Dial Leroi Rupert, DJ*. New York: Lothrop. (I)

Gioffre, M. (1985). *Starstruck*. New York: Scholastic/Apple. (I)

Goffstein, M. B. (1972). *A little Schubert*. New York: Harper & Row. (P)

Greenfield, E. (1988). *Nathaniel talking*. New York: Writers & Readers. (I, MC)

Griffith, H., & Stevenson, J. (1986). *Georgia music*. New York: Greenwillow. (P)

Grimm, J., & Grimm, W. (E. Shub & J. Domanska, Trans.). (1980). *The Brementown musicians*. New York: Greenwillow. (P)

Haas, I. (1981). *The little moon theater*. New York: Atheneum. (P)

Hantzig, D. (1989). *Pied piper of Hamlin*. New York: Random House. (P)

Hasley, D., & Gammel, S. (1983). *The old banjo*. New York: Macmillan. (P)

Hedderwick, M. (1985). *Katie Morag and the two grandmothers*. London: The Bodley Head. (P)

Hentoff, N. (1965). *Jazz country*. New York: Harper & Row. (I, MC)

Hilgartner, B. (1986). *A murder for her majesty*. Boston: Houghton Mifflin. (I)

Hill, D. (1978). *Ms. Glee was waiting*. New York: Atheneum. (I)

Hoban, R. (1976). *A bargain for Frances*. New York: Harper & Row. (P)

Hoffman, E. T., & Sendak, M. (1984). *The nutcracker*. New York: Crown. (P, I)

Hogrogian, N. (1973). *The cat who loved to sing*. Palmer, AK: Aladdin. (P)

Hughes, S. (1983). *Alfie gives a hand*. New York: Mulberry Book. (P)

Isadora, R. (1979). *Ben's trumpet*. New York: Greenwillow. (P, MC)

Jeffers, S. (1974). *All the pretty horses*. New York: Macmillan. (P)

Johnson, J. W. (1976). *God's trombones*. New York: Viking/Penguin. (I)

Johnston, T., & dePaola, T. (1988). *Pages of music*. New York: G. P. Putnam's Sons. (P)

Kherdian, D., & Hogrogian, N. (1990). *The cat's midsummer jamboree*. New York: G. P. Putnam's Sons. (P)

Komaiko, L., & Westman, B. (1987). *I like music*. New York: Harper & Row. (P)

Kroll, S., & Lobel, A. (1988). *Looking for Daniela*. New York: Holiday House. (P)

Kuskin, K., & Simont, M. (1982). *The philharmonic gets dressed*. New York: Harper & Row. (P)

Leodhas, S. N., & Hogrogiam, N. (1965). *Always room for one more*. New York: Henry Holt. (P)

Lionni, L. (1979). *Geraldine, the music mouse*. New York: Random House. (P)

Lisle, J. T. (1986). *Sirens and spies*. New York: Bradbury. (I)

MacLachlan, P. (1988). *The facts and fictions of Minna Pratt*. New York: Harper & Row. (I)

Martin, B., Archambault, J., & Rand, T. (1986). *Barn dance*. New York: Henry Holt. (P)

Martin, B., Archambault, J., & Endicott, J. (1988). *Listen to the rain*. New York: Henry Holt. (P)

Martin, B., & Rand, T. (1988). *Up and down on the merry-go-round*. New York: Henry Holt. (P)

Maxner, J., & Joyce, W. (1989). *Nicholas cricket*. New York: Harper & Row. (P)

Mayer, M. (1974). *Frog goes to dinner*. New York: Scholastic. (P)

McCuffrey, A. (1976). *Dragonsong*. New York: Macmillan. (I)

Menotti, G., & Lemieux, M. (1986). *Amahl and the night visitors*. New York: Morrow. (I, MC)

Newton, S. (1983). *I will call it Georgie's blues*. New York: Viking. (I)

Paterson, K. (1985). *Come sing, Jimmy Jo*. New York: Dutton. (I)

Paulsen, G. (1985). *Dogsong*. New York: Bradbury. (I)

Pinkwater, D. (1976). *Lizard music*. New York: Dodd Mead. (I)

Rylant, C., & Gammell, S. (1985). *The relatives came*. New York: Bradbury. (P)

Sage, J. (1991). *The little band*. New York: Macmillan Child Group. (P)

Schick, E. (1977). *One summer night*. New York: Greenwillow. (P)

Schick, E. (1984). *A piano for Julie*. New York: Greenwillow. (P)

Schroeder, A., & Fuchs, B. (1989). *Ragtime tumpie*. Boston: Little, Brown. (P, MC)

Shannon, G., Aruego, J., & Dewey, A. (1981). *Lizard's song*. New York: Greenwillow. (P)

Sharmat, M. (1991). *Nate the great and musical note*. New York: Dell. (P)

Showell, E. (1983). *Cecelia and the Blue Mountain boy*. New York: Lothrop. (I)

Skofield, J., & Gundersheimer, D. (1981). *Night dances*. New York: Harper & Row. (P)

Stock, C. (1988). *Sophie's knapsack*. New York: Lothrop. (P)

Thomas, I. (1981). *Willie blows a mean horn*. New York: Harper & Row. (P)

Treschel, G. (1992). *The lute's tune*. New York: Doubleday. (P)

Turkle, B. (1968). *The fiddler of high lonesome*. New York: Viking. (I)

Voight, C. (1983). *Dicey's song*. New York: Atheneum. (I)

Walter, M. (1989). *Mariah loves rock*. New York: Macmillan. (I, MC)

Walter, M. P., & Tomes, M. (1980). *Ty's one-man band*. New York: Scholastic. (P)

Weik, M. H., & Grifalconi, A. (1966). *The jazz man*. New York: Atheneum. (P, MC)

Wharton, T. (1991). *Hildegard sings*. New York: Farrar, Straus, & Giroux. (P)

Williams, V. B. (1983). *Something special for me*. New York: Greenwillow. (P)

Wood, A., Wood, A., & Wood, D. (1988). *Elbert's bad word*. New York: Harcourt Brace Jovanovich. (P)

Yolen, J. (1983). *Commander toad and the big black hole*. New York: G. P. Putnam's Sons. (P)

Yorinks, A., & Egielski, S. (1988). *Bravo, Minsky!* New York: Farrar, Straus & Giroux. (P)

Zolotow, C., & Tafuri, N. (1982). *The song*. New York: Greenwillow. (P)

Music History and Appreciation

Anderson, D. (1982). *The piano makers*. New York: Pantheon. (I)

Arnold, C. (1985). *Music lessons for Alex*. New York: Clarion. (P)

Autexier, P. (1992). *Beethoven, the composer as hero*. New York: Abrams. (I)

Bain, G., & Leather, M. (1986). *The picture life of Bruce Springsteen*. New York: Franklin Watts. (I)

Bayless, K., & Ramsey, M. (1990). *Music: A way of life for the young child*. New York: Merrill/Macmillan. (P)

Berliner, D. C. (1961). *All about the orchestra and what it plays*. New York: Random House. (I)

Bierhorst, J. (1979). *A cry from the earth: Music of the North American Indians*. New York: Four Winds. (I, MC)

Brighton, C. (1990). *Mozart: Scenes from the childhood of the composer*. New York: Doubleday. (I)

Busnar, G. (1979). *It's rock and roll*. New York: Julian Messner. (I)

Downing, J. (1990). *Mozart tonight*. New York: Julian Messner. (I)

Englander, R. (1983). *Opera! What's all the screaming about?* New York: Walker. (I)

English, B. L. (1980). *You can't be timid with a trumpet*. New York: Lothrop. (I)

Fornatale, P. (1987). *The story of rock n' roll*. New York: Morrow. (I)

Gass, I. (1970). *Mozart: Child wonder, child composer*. New York: Lothrop. (I)

Glass, P. (1969). *Singing soldiers: A history of the Civil War in song*. New York: Grosset & Dunlap. (I)

Hargrove, J. *Pablo Casals*. Chicago: Children's Press. (I)

Haskins, J. (1986). *Diana Ross: Star supreme*. New York: Puffin. (I, MC)

Haskins, J. (1987). *Black music in America*. New York: Crowell. (I, MC)

Helprin, M., & Van Allsburg, C. (1990). *Swan lake*. Boston: Houghton Mifflin. (I)

Hughes, L. (1982). *Jazz*. New York: Watts. (I, MC)

Lasker, D., & Lasker, J. (1979). *The boy who loved music*. New York: Viking. (I)

Monjo, F. N., & Brenner, F. (1975). *Letters to Horseface: Being the story of Wolfgang Amadeus Mozart's journey to Italy*. New York: Viking. (I)

Previn, A. (Ed.). (1983). *Andre Previn's guide to the orchestra*. New York: G. P. Putnam's Sons. (I)

Price, L. (1990). *Aida: A picture book for all ages*. San Diego: Harcourt Brace Jovanovich. (I)

Rosenberg, J. (1989). *Sing me a song: Metropolitan Opera's book of opera stories for children*. New York: Thames & Hudson. (I)

Schaff, P. (1980). *The violin close up*. New York: Four Winds. (I)

Stevens, B. (1983). *Ben Franklin's glass harmonica*. Minneapolis: Carolrhoda. (P)

Stevens, B. (1991). *Handel and the famous sword swallower of Halle*. New York: Philomel. (I)

Suggs, W. W., & Arno, E. (1971). *Meet the orchestra*. New York: Macmillan. (I)

Terkel, S. (1975). *Giants of jazz*. New York: Crowell. (I, MC)

Weil, L. (1989). *The magic of music*. New York: Holiday House. (I)

Weil, L. (1982). *Wolferl: The first six years in the life of Wolfgang Mozart*. New York: Holiday House. (I)

Willson, R. (1991). *Mozart's story*. London: A. & C. Black. (I)

POETRY

Abercrombie, B. (Ed.). (1977). *The other side of a poem*. Scranton, PA: Harper & Row. (P, I)

Adams, A. (1972). *Poetry of earth*. New York: Scribner. (P, I)

Adoff, A. (1974). *My black me: A beginning book of black poetry*. New York: Dutton. (P, I, MC)

Adoff, A. (1975). *Black out loud*. New York: Dell. (P, I, MC)

Adoff, A. (1976). *Big sister tells me that I'm black*. New York: Henry Holt. (P, I, MC)

Adoff, A. (1981). *OUTside, INside poems*. New York: Lathrop. (P, I, MC)

Adoff, A. (1982). *All the colors of the race*. New York: Lathrop. (P, I, MC)

Aiken, C. (1965). *Cats and bats and things with wings*. New York: Atheneum. (P, I)

Arico, D. (1990). *Easter treasures: Stories and poems of the season*. New York: Doubleday. (P, I)

Arnold, T. (1990). *Mother Goose's words of wit and wisdom*. New York: Dial. (P)

Aylesworth, J. (1990). *The completed hickory dickory dock*. New York: Atheneum. (P)

Behm, H. (1992). *Trees*. New York: Henry Holt. (P)

Brewton, S., & Brewton, J. (Eds.). (1973). *My tung's tungled and other ridiculous situations*. New York: Thomas Crowell. (P, I)

Brown, R. (1988). *Ladybug, ladybug*. New York: Dutton Children's Books. (P)

Bunting, E. (1991). *In the haunted house*. New York: Clarion. (I)

Carle, E. (1989). *Animals, animals*. New York: Philomel. (P, I)

Carle, E. (1992). *Dragons, dragons, and other creatures that never were*. New York: G. P. Putnam's Sons. (P, I)

Ciardi, J. (1959). *The reason for the pelican*. Philadelphia: J. B. Lippincott. (P)

Ciardi, J. (1962). *You read to me, I'll read to you*. Philadelphia: J. B. Lippincott. (P, I)

Ciardi, J. (1985). *Doodle soup*. Boston: Houghton Mifflin. (P, I)

Clark, A. (1991). *In my mother's house*. New York: Viking/Children's Books. (P, MC)

Clifton, L. (1974). *Everett Anderson's year*. New York: Henry Holt. (I)

Cole, J. (1984). *A new treasury of children's poetry*. New York: Doubleday. (P, I)

Cole, J. (1990). *Anna Banana: 101 jump-rope rhymes*. New York: Morrow. (I, MC)

Cole, J., & Calmenson, S. (1990). *"Miss Mary Mack" and other children's street rhymes*. Long Beach, CA: BeechTree Books. (I, MC)

Cole, W. (1964). *Beastly boys and ghostly girls*. New York: World. (P, I)

Cole, W. (1966). *Oh! what nonsense!* New York: Viking. (P, I)

Cullum, A. (1971). *The geranium on the windowsill just died, but teacher you went right on*. New York: Harlin Books. (P, I)

Dakos, K. (1991). *If you're not here, please raise your hand: Poems about school*. New York: Four Winds. (P, I)

De Gerez, T. (1984). *My song is a piece of jade: Spanish/English poetry*. Boston: Little, Brown. (P, I, MC)

de Regniers, B. (1991). *Sing a song of popcorn*. New York: Scholastic. (P)

Dickinson, E. (1987). *Acts of light*. Boston: Bullfinch. (P, I)

Dickinson, E. (1990). *A brighter garden*. New York: Philomel. (P, I)

Dunbar, P. (1978). *I greet the dawn*. New York: Atheneum. (P, I)

Dunning, S. (Ed.). (1969). *Reflections on a gift of watermelon pickle*. New York: Lothrop. (P, I)

Dunning, S. (Ed.). (1969). *Some haystacks don't even have any needles*. New York: Lothrop. (P, I)

Durrell, A., & Sachs, M. (1990). *The big book for peace*. New York: Dutton Children's Books. (P, I)

Fleischman, P. (1985). *I am phoenix: Poems for two voices*. New York: Harper & Row. (P, I)

Fleischman, P. (1992). *Joyful noise: Poems for two voices.* New York: Harper Collins Children's Books. (P, I)

Frank, J. (1969). *Poems to read to the very young.* New York: Random House. (P)

Frank, J. (Ed.). (1973). *Snow toward evening: A year in a river valley.* New York: Dial. (P, I)

Frost, R. (1969). *You come, too.* New York: Holt, Rinehart, & Winston. (P, I)

Frost, R. (1988). *Birches.* New York: Holt, Rinehart, & Winston. (P, I)

Fufuka, K. (1975). *"My daddy is a cool dude" and other poems.* New York: Dial. (P, I, MC)

Fujikawa, G. (1969). *A child's book of poems.* New York: Grosset & Dunlap. (P, I)

Garden, G. (1989). *The skylighters.* New York: Oxford University Press. (P, I)

Gerrard, R. (1992). *A pocket full of posies.* New York: Farrar, Straus, & Giroux. (P, I)

Giovanni, N. (1971). *Spin a soft black song: Poems for children.* New York: Hill & Wong. (P, I, MC)

Giovanni, N. (1973). *Ego tripping and other poems for young people.* Wichita, KS: Lawrence Hill. (P, I, MC)

Goldstein, B. (1988). *Bear in mind: A book of bear poems.* New York: Viking Children's Books. (P)

Greenberg, K. (1988) *Rap.* Minneapolis: Lerner. (I, MC)

Greenfield, E. (1978). *Honey I love.* New York: Thomas Crowell. (P, I, MC)

Grimes, N. (1986). *Something on my mind.* New York: Dial. (P, I, MC)

Heller, R. (1984). *Plants that never ever bloom.* New York: G. P. Putnam's Sons. (P, I)

Heller, R. (1991). *Merry-go-round: A book about nouns.* New York: Grosset & Dunlap. (P, I)

Higginson, W. (1991). *Wind in the long grass: A collection of haiku.* New York: Simon & Schuster. (P, I, MC)

Hopkins, L. (Ed.). (1970). *The city spreads its wings.* New York: Franklin Watts. (P, I)

Hughes, L. (1969). *Don't you turn back.* New York: Alfred Knopf. (P, I)

Janeczko, P. (Ed.). (1991). *The place my words are looking for: What poets say about and through their work.* New York: Bradbury. (I)

Johnston, T. (1980). *I'm gonna tell mama I want an Iguana.* New York: Putnam Publishing Group. (P)

Koch, K., & Farrell, K. (1985). *Talking to the sun: An illustrated anthology of poems for young people.* New York: Henry Holt. (P, I)

Larche, D. (1985). *Father Gander nursery rhymes.* Santa Barbara, CA: Advocacy Press. (P)

Larrick, N. (Ed.). (1968). *On city streets.* New York: M. Evans. (P, I)

Larrick, N. (1972). *Let's do a poem.* New York: Doubleday. (P, I)

Larrick, N. (1988). *Cats.* New York: Philomel. (P, I)

Larrick, N. (1990). *Mice are nice.* New York: Philomel. (P)

Lear, E. (1951). *Complete nonsense of Edward Lear.* New York: Dover. (P, I)

Lear, E. (1992). *A was once an apple pie.* Cambridge, MA: Candlewick. (P)

Lester, J. (1974). *Who am I?* New York: Dial. (P)

Leuders, E. (Ed.). (1976). *Zero makes me hungry.* New York: Lothrop. (P)

Lewis, J. P. (1992). *Earth verses and water rhymes.* New York: Macmillan. (P, I)

Lewis, J. P. (1992). *Two-legged, four-legged, no-legged rhymes.* New York: Alfred Knopf. (P)

Lewis, R. (1966). *Miracles: Poems by children of the English-speaking world.* New York: Simon & Schuster. (P, I)

Livingston, M. (1980). *There was a place and other poems.* New York: Holiday House. (P, I)

Livingston, M. (1982). *No way of knowing: Dallas poems.* New York: Atheneum. (P, I)

Livingston, M. (1985). *Poem-making.* New York: Holiday House. (P, I)

Livingston, M. (1987). *Cat poems.* Boston: Holiday House. (P, I)

Manguel, A. (1991). *Seasons.* New York: Doubleday. (P)

Martin, B., Jr. (1989). *Chicka, chicka, boom, boom.* New York: Simon & Schuster. (P, I, MC)

Martin, B., Jr., & Archaubault, J. (1987). *Here are my hands*. New York: Henry Holt. (P, MC)

Martin, B., Jr. & Archaubault, J. (1988). *Listen to the rain*. New York: Holt, Rinehart, & Winston. (P)

Marzollo, J. (1990). *Pretend you're a cat*. New York: Dial. (P)

McCord, D. (1967). *Every time I climb a tree*. Boston: Little, Brown. (P, I)

Merriam, E. (1964). *It doesn't always have to rhyme*. New York: Atheneum. (P, I)

Merriam, E. (1986). *Fresh paint*. Riverside, NJ: Macmillan. (P, I)

Michels, B., & White, B. (Eds.). (1983). *Apples on a stick: The folklore of black children*. New York: Coward. (P, I, MC)

Milne, A. A. (1975). *Now we are six*. New York: Dell. (P)

Nerlove, M. (1990). *If all the world were paper*. Nills, IL: Whitman. (P, I)

Ness, E. (1975). *"Amelia mixed up the mustard" and other poems*. New York: Scribner's. (P, I)

O'Neill, M. (1989). *Hailstones and halibut bones*. New York: Doubleday. (P, I)

Prelutsky, J. (1983). *The Random House book of poetry for children*. New York: Random House. (P, I)

Prelutsky, J. (1985). *For laughing out loud*. New York: Greenwillow. (P)

Prelutsky, J. (1988). *Tyrannosaurus was a beast*. New York: Greenwillow. (P)

Prelutsky, J. (1990). *Poems of A. Nanny Mouse*. New York: Alfred Knopf. (P)

Prelutsky, J. (1990). *Something big has been here*. New York: Greenwillow. (P)

Sandburg, C. (1984). *Rainbows are made*. Orlando, FL: Harcourt Brace Jovanovich. (P, I)

Schwartz, A. (1992). *And the green grass grew all around: Folk poetry for everyone*. New York: Harper Collins. (P, I, MC)

Sendak, M. (1970). *Chicken soup with rice*. New York: Scholastic. (P)

Serfozo, M. (1990). *Rain talk*. New York: Macmillan Child Group. (P, I)

Siebert, D. (1988). *Mojave*. New York: Harper Trophy. (P, I, MC)

Silverstein, S. (1974). *Where the sidewalk ends*. Scranton, PA: Harper & Row. (P, I)

Steele, M. (1991). *Anna's garden songs*. New York: Scholastic. (P, I)

Stopple, L. (1975). *A box of peppermints*. Austin, TX: American Universal Artforms. (P, I)

Strickland, D. (1986). *Listen children: An anthology of black literature*. New York: Bantam. (I, MC)

Whybrow, J. (1992). *Quacky quack-quack*. New York: Macmillan. (P)

Willard, N. (1980). *A visit to William Blake's inn*. San Diego: Harcourt Brace Jovanovich. (I)

Wyndham, R. (1968). *Chinese Mother Goose rhymes*. Cleveland, OH: World. (P, MC)

Yolen, J. (1992). *Street rhymes around the world*. Honesdale, PA: Wordsong. (I, MC)

PHOTOGRAPHY

Allen, M., & Rotner, S. (1991). *Changes*. New York: Macmillan Children's Book Group. (P)

Arnold, C. (1991). *Snake*. New York: Morrow Junior Books. (P, I)

Barrett, N. (1988). *Pandas*. New York: Watts. (P, I)

Behrens, J. (1986). *Fiesta*. San Francisco: Children's Book Pr. (P, MC)

Brenner, B. (1973). *Bodies*. New York: Dutton. (P, MC)

Brown, T. (1986). *Hello, amigos*. New York: Henry Holt. (P, MC)

Brown, T. (1987). *Chinese New Year*. New York: Henry Holt. (P, MC)

Burton, J. (1991). See How They Grow series. *Kitten* (1991); *Puppy* (1991). New York: Lodestar. (P)

Cobb, V. (1990). *Natural Wonders*. New York: Lothrop. (P, I)

Cornish, S. (1974). *Grandmother's pictures*. Freeport, ME: Bookstore Press. (P)

Cousteau Society series (1992). *Dolphins; Penguins; Seals; Turtles.* New York: Simon & Schuster. (P, I)

Doubilet, A. (1991). *Under the sea from A to Z.* New York: Crown. (P)

Eye Openers series (1991). *Baby animals; Jungle animals; Pets; Zoo animals.* New York: Aladdin. (P)

Feeney, S. (1980). *A is for aloha.* Honolulu: University Press of Hawaii. (P, MC)

Feeney, S. (1985). *Hawaii is a rainbow.* Honolulu: University Press of Hawaii. (P, MC)

Freedman, R. (1988). *Lincoln: A photobiography.* New York: Clarion. (I)

Goldsmith, D. (1992). *Hoang Auk: A Vietnamese-American boy.* New York: Holiday House. (I, MC)

Grillone, L., & Gennaro, J. (1978). *Small worlds close up.* (P, I)

Hewett, J. (1990). *Hector lives in the United States now: The story of a Mexican-American child.* New York: Lippincott. (I, MC)

Hirschi, R. (1990). *Winter.* New York: Dutton Children's Books. (P)

Hirschi, R. (1990). *Spring.* New York: Dutton Children's Books. (P)

Hirschi, R. (1991). *Fall.* New York: Dutton Children's Books. (P)

Hoban, T. (1985). *A children's zoo.* New York: Greenwillow. (P)

Hoban, T. (1985). *Is it larger? Is it smaller?* New York: Greenwillow. (P)

Hoban, T. (1990). *Exactly the opposite.* New York: Greenwillow (P).

Kuklin, S. (1991). *How my family lives in America.* New York: Bradbury. (P, MC)

Lehrman, F. (1990). *Loving the earth: A sacred landscape book for children.* Berkeley, CA: Celestial Arts. (P, I)

Meltzer, M. (1986). *Dorothea Lange: Life through the camera.* New York: Piffin. (I)

Miller, M. (1991). *Whose shoe.* New York: Greenwillow. (P)

Morris, A. (1989). *Bread, bread, bread.* New York: Lothrop, Lee, & Shepard. (P, I, MC)

Morris, A. (1989). *Hats, hats, hats.* New York: Lothrop, Lee, & Shepard. (P, I, MC)

Morris, A. (1990). *Loving.* New York: Lothrop, Lee, & Shepard. (P, I, MC)

Oliver, S. (1990). *My first look at seasons.* New York: Random House. (P)

Rauzon, M. (1992). *Jungles.* New York: Doubleday. (I)

Ricklin, N. (1988). *Grandpa and me.* New York: Simon & Schuster. (P)

Robbins, K. (1991) *Bridges.* New York: Dial. (P, I)

Schlein, M. (1990). *Elephants.* New York: Aladdin. (I)

Schlein, M. (1990). *Gorillas.* New York: Aladdin. (I)

Steichen, E. (1985, 30th Anniversary Ed.). *The family of man.* New York: Museum of Modern Art. (P, I, MC)

Waters, K., & Slorenz-Low, M. (1990). *Lion dancer: Earnie Wan's Chinese New Year.* New York: Scholastic. (P, MC)

Wilkes, A. (1991). *My first green book.* New York: Alfred Knopf. (P)

Author Index

Subject Index